LET'S *dance*

A HANDBOOK FOR TEACHERS

LET'S *dance*

A HANDBOOK FOR TEACHERS

Mary Harlow

Linda Rolfe

The authors wish to thank all the teachers and colleagues who helped with the development of this book, especially the following: Jacqueline Smith for her continued guidance and interest in our work, Chris Buckley, Paul Buckley and Phil Burner of Combe Down Primary School, Rebecca Trevor, Sarah Hennessy, Elspeth Davis, Sarah Miller and Julie Beckett.

They would also like to acknowledge the Kinesis Dance Company (Rowan Ayton, Leona Farquharson, Rebecca Fox, Kelly Green, Katie Moon, Louise O'Sullivan, Heidi Whitehead, Sally Wilmer, Zöe Wilmer), the children in the photographs – Ryan Buckley, Katie Buswell, Tom Curtis, Lloyd Davies, Lowri Davies, Fiona Fitzpatrick, Simon Francis, Rhianan Jones, Amber Khan, Victoria Lloyd, Claire Morris, Jessica Rees, Leanda Richards, Yee Yan Yip and last, but certainly not least, the children who they have worked with throughout the years, for it is the children who have contributed most to the practical development of their ideas in dance.

This book is dedicated to our parents and families who have supported us throughout our work.

Published by BBC Educational Publishing,
a division of BBC Enterprises Limited,
80 Wood Lane, London W12 0TT

© BBC Enterprises Limited/Linda Rolfe and Mary Harlow
ISBN 0563 35014 8

Reprinted 1993

Designer: Claire Robertson
Photographer: Chris Fairclough
Illustrator: David Downton
Copy Editor: Sarah Harland

Photograph acknowledgements:

Catherine Ashmore, p. 11; Baron, Hulton Deutsch Collection, p. 10; Luke Finn, BBC, p. 14; Hulton Deutsch Collection, p. 10; The Kobal Collection, p. 10; Chris Nash, AMP, p. 11; Honey Salvadori, Network Photographers, p. 10; F. Walther, ZEFA, p. 11; ZEFA, p. 11.

This book is set in 12/15 pt Sabon roman

Typeset by Goodfellow & Egan, Cambridge
Printed by Clays Ltd, St Ives plc

Contents

foreword

I have known Mary Harlow and Linda Rolfe for many years and value highly what they have achieved in their work with young people and teachers in dance in education. Their unstinted endeavours have resulted in the county of Avon gaining a position of national recognition for the strength and quality of its dance in education. The energy, enthusiasm and dedication they convey to pupils and teachers always results in very happy and fruitful experiences for all who participate in their dance courses.

Through participation in many national conferences and active membership of the National Dance Teachers' Association, Mary Harlow and Linda Rolfe are fully aware of the current developments and concerns in dance education. Indeed, they are part of the team who advised the Department of Education and Science Working Group for Physical Education prior to publication of the proposals for Physical Education in the National Curriculum in 1991. It is from their knowledge of the needs of teachers, particularly the non-specialist teachers in primary schools, that the idea for this book emerged.

In my view, the book appears as a most timely and relevant aid for teachers who will have the daunting problem of interpreting the very brief statutory orders for Dance within Physical Education. The few short statements on content for Dance in the form of programmes of study at the key stages, leave most non-specialist teachers completely at a loss. The need for in-service training is paramount, but a day course here and there only works if teachers have texts to reinforce and clarify what they have learned. This book offers much to teachers in that it will make clear, reinforce and augment initial or in-service course content. But it also provides a very sound basis for those with a little knowledge to progress and advance their own teaching confidently. Until the publication of this book, no texts exist to back-up teacher training specifically for Dance in the National Curriculum.

The content of the book is presented in logically ordered sections to help teachers understand the various types of Dance, its distinctiveness and the contribution Dance can make in the education and development of children, and the ways in which syllabuses and schemes of work can be designed. There follows a multitude of material for teaching, lesson plans and very useful suggestions on methodology and assessment. The underlying principle that Dance experiences, like experiences in the other arts, should develop pupils artistically and aesthetically is dominant throughout the book. Clearly, teachers who use this book will gain a very secure understanding of how to teach dance employing the three activities of performing, creating and appreciating dances.

Dance education suffers from a dearth of literature. We need inspiring and experienced teachers such as Mary Harlow and Linda Rolfe to fill the gap. This they do admirably. I thank them and welcome this excellent book and I know that I speak for many teachers too.

Jacqueline Smith-Autard
Bedford, 1992

preface

This book has been written for teachers who wish to increase their knowledge and understanding about the nature of dance and how it can contribute to children's education. Every child should be provided with the opportunity to have a dance education and, with this aim in mind, the text seeks to provide *all* teachers with the skills to plan and deliver a broad and balanced dance curriculum. Guided by the structure provided in the statutory programme of study for dance in the National Curriculum for Physical Education the book focuses on the artistic and aesthetic education of children learning *in* and *through* dance. Its content includes subject knowledge related to composing, performing and viewing dances, together with practical ideas and lesson plans designed to guide and assist the teaching of dance in schools.

We hope that teachers will take this material, adapt, modify and develop it to suit their needs and those of their children. Through this process they may sense some of the excitement and challenge that can be found through teaching dance. The intrinsic satisfaction gained by providing children with ways of becoming educated in dance will provide many rewards.

Linda Rolfe . Mary Harlow

SECTION ONE

The Development of Dance in Schools

WHAT IS *dance?*

Dance is fun, giving pleasure and joy; it lifts the spirit and stimulates the mind. It is a wonderful way of developing our natural movement potential as an expressive medium. Dance speaks a very special language which enables us to communicate with others, to understand more about ourselves and the world around us.

Dance is the fastest growing performing art in today's society. This explosion of interest in dance is witnessed by the increase in small touring dance companies, greater media coverage of dance, the revival of community classes, the emergence of youth dance groups, the development of extensive vocational opportunities and the tremendous growth in theatre audiences.

Throughout our history dance has served many different purposes all of which are evident today. Dance is perceived as a:

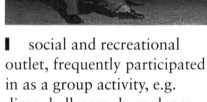

▮ physical activity, e.g. dance exercise classes, tap, jazz

▮ popular entertainment with wide appeal, e.g. musical, pop video dances

▮ social and recreational outlet, frequently participated in as a group activity, e.g. disco, ballroom, barn dance

▮ form of religious worship and as a part of cultural rituals, e.g. Greek wedding dance, Asian temple dance

▮ means of expressing national or tribal loyalty, e.g. traditional folk dance, street carnivals

▮ means of education within a society exploring the cultural place of dance alongside the other arts

▮ an art form – where it provides a means of expression and communication with an audience.

▮ dance therapy offering emotional and physical benefits to both participants or an audience

▮ profession, e.g. choreographer, teacher, performer

In spite of the diverse nature of dance, it has certain common characteristics. Dance:

▮ uses the human body

▮ extends through time – this may vary from a few moments to several hours

▮ exists in space, whether it takes place in a school hall, through village streets or on a stage

▮ is rhythmically patterned, and frequently has some type of auditory accompaniment, e.g. clapping, singing or music

▮ usually intends to communicate, whether it is the expression of conflict in a contemporary dance work, the physical exuberance of a tap dance, or the narrative in a ballet

▮ frequently has a characteristic movement style and is structured into a particular form, e.g. in social dance the Samba is recognisably different from the Waltz, traditional Asian dance forms bear little resemblance to the Russian Cossack dance.

Whether dance has as its **primary** purpose either **performance** or **participation** will depend upon the circumstances and situation in which it is taking place. On some occasions the two may merge as an audience joins with the dancers and enters into the performance.

Quotes from Children

According to children, dance is:

You can dance about anything
Kate

I like doing it for fun
Rajni

When I used to think about dance I thought you just moved to the music, there's a lot more to it than that
Ruth

Dance encourages me to do something I wouldn't normally do with someone I didn't even know
Rory

Dance is like a bubble bursting in your tummy
Gemma

In the future I might be a dancer
Joseph

I like dance because it always makes you think about how you feel
Hayden

I would like to show my work to other children in other schools
Kamaljit

Hard work but better than anything
Tom

When I dance it makes me feel more confident
Tony

Dance is not just for dancers it's for everybody
Leona

THE DEVELOPMENT OF DANCE IN *education*

The exciting revival in dance has been mirrored within education. During the past two decades dance in education has made swift and impressive progress. It has radically changed from what could be described as creative movement in which the pupils could do their own thing, to more structured experiences whereby pupils come to know and understand dance as an art form in all its cultural contexts.

In the National Curriculum dance appears as a distinct aspect of the Physical Education programme, where it is recognised as an art:

'. . . of all the activities in Physical Education only dance as an art form in its own right is characterised by the intention and ability to make symbolic statements to create meaning. This . . . distinguishes dance from other physical activities and shares characteristics with music, drama and art. These art forms are the basis for children's artistic education. . .'

(*Physical Education 5–16*, DES August 1991, p. 64)

Arts education enables children to develop a wide range of their intellectual capabilities *in* and *through* a variety of disciplines. These provide children with special ways of using their imagination to explore and make sense of their experiences.

In the arts, aesthetic development is concerned with deepening children's sensitivities to the pleasures and meanings of the arts. It involves heightening sensory awareness, developing perceptual skills, encouraging personal interpretation and critical reflection. By appraising and becoming sensitive to the work of others, the arts help children to understand their culture and extends their artistic experience and judgement. These aspects of aesthetic and cultural development have value both within and beyond arts activity. As such, they form an essential component of a balanced education.

WHY *dance?*

The distinct contribution of dance to children's artistic education

Through dance as Art Education, dance:

▌ provides children with opportunities for their natural joy and delight in expressive movement to be developed into dance forms

▌ develops children's use of imagination and non-verbal communication through movement

▌ allows children to explore and structure their ideas and feelings through movement

▌ encourages children to acquire technical and performing skills focusing on the expressive qualities of movement

▌ gives children access to a distinct form of knowledge and understanding through:

● introducing children to a variety of dance forms such as Theatre, Social and Traditional, within a cultural context

● encouraging children to be sensitive and perceptive to meaning in dance

The contribution of dance to other curriculum areas

Dance:

▌ provides opportunities for the development of personal and social skills through individual and group work

▌ gives insight into different cultural traditions

▌ promotes a positive attitude to health and fitness through the development of co-ordination, strength, stamina and suppleness

▌ reinforces the cross-curricular nature of learning within thematic and topic work

▌ encourages the exploration of beliefs, attitudes and values within society

▌ acts as a catalyst for project work, language development, problem solving experiences, independent and collaborative teaching and learning styles

▌ establishes community links through theatre visits, the involvement of professional artistes and the use of local arts centres and agencies

▌ creates vocational and training opportunities

Dance is part of the National Curriculum requirements and alongside all the arts has a vital role to play in children's education. It is, therefore, essential for schools to design a policy statement for the arts which includes a rationale for the teaching of dance. This should clearly articulate the educational value of dance and what constitutes a balanced, dance education.

ASPECTS OF DANCE *education*

The essential premise for dance teaching is centred upon pupils coming to know and understand dance through:

▌ *Performing dance*
▌ *Creating dance* and
▌ *Viewing dance*

in all its contexts.

In a well-structured Dance Education, equal attention must be given to these three interrelated strands and children should be encouraged to acquire the appropriate skills and knowledge related to individual aspects.

The three components – Performance, Composition and Appreciation provide the basis for the various established syllabi including GCSE, A level, BTEC, Pre-Vocational Training, Diploma and Higher Degree courses in dance.

Dance Performance

Today it is clearly recognised that dance is a performing art, and as in music and drama, performance is an important aspect of dance education.

Performance gives young people the opportunity to assess the effectiveness of the dances they have composed or learned and to share these with their peers or a wider audience. Pupils should be encouraged to see their performance in terms of both personal attainment and presentation for an audience.

The youngest of school children already possess a great range of natural movements and expressive ability. Many have even acquired an elementary sense of aesthetic awareness of movement; they will consciously, and with pleasure, move fluently, lightly, rhythmically, expressively and with an emerging sense of form.

In an early years dance programme children's joy, delight and satisfaction in expressive movement should be harnessed and learning opportunities designed to challenge and exploit this potential. The mastery of basic technical skills are essential to enable them to move with ease and precision, allowing them to release their individuality in imaginative situations. Initial teaching should endeavour to focus on the improvement of balance, control, co-ordination and posture, and the rhythmic, spatial and dynamic features of movements need to be constantly stressed. An introduction to more specific forms of social, theatre and traditional dance at this stage will enable the children to become competent in a range of dance styles and techniques. In later years emphasis should be placed on more complex elements of technical accomplishment and opportunities provided for children to experience specific styles through use of professional artistes and specialist teachers.

Dance Composition

Children need to be given the knowledge of how to create, shape and structure dance ideas into expressive dance forms. Young children often appear to be conscious of the qualities of their movement and gestures and, with a little encouragement, will play and improvise with such basic dance ingredients. It is the aim of dance education in the early years to foster and develop all these natural abilities by providing opportunities for pupils to create or compose simple dance sequences through improvisation, interaction with one another and with sensitive teacher direction. As pupils' knowledge, understanding and skills develop they become able to compose dances of increasing complexity and sophistication, showing evidence of, for example, formal qualities – beginnings, developments, contrasts and resolutions.

Dance Appreciation

From the earliest years the dance programme will encourage children to view each other's work and make discerning remarks; it is by drawing attention to the aesthetic qualities of movement that the first lessons in aesthetic appreciation begin. The teacher comments upon, for example, the line of a leap, nimble footwork, delicacy of contrast, intricacy of pattern, effortlessness and ease, as well as the dramatic qualities of perceived power, tension, resolution and suspense. These observed distinctions are the beginnings of critical artistic appreciation in dance.

The teacher's appraisals will play an important part in aesthetic development and will be applied initially with a desire to encourage in a formative and supportive way. As critical ability increases, pupils will be expected to discern, with growing accuracy and sensitivity, the contextual features which characterise different aspects of choreography – distinctiveness in style and technique – which will become the objects of perceptive description, analysis, interpretation and evaluation. These categories of appreciation will be applied to the children's own work, to the works of professional choreographers and to the appreciation of social, theatre and traditional forms of dance within a cultural context.

At all levels a comprehensive dance programme should:

▌ consist of the activities of composing, performing and appreciating in a *variety* of contexts

▌ be for *all* children.

SECTION TWO

The Contents of the Dance Curriculum

The teaching of dance is centred upon children coming to know and understand dance as a performing art through *Performing, Creating* or *Composing* and *Viewing* Dances. In a well-structured dance education equal attention needs to be given to each of these three interrelated strands, so that children learn to appreciate dance.

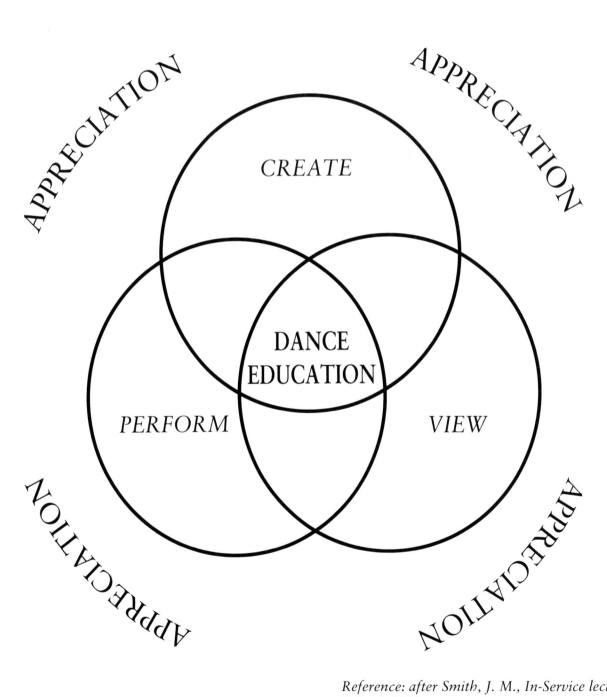

Reference: after Smith, J. M., In-Service lecture, Bristol, 1989

PERFORMING *d**ance**

The mastery of basic technical skills is essential to enable children to move with ease and precision. This will allow them to respond imaginatively and provide them with the expressive movement skills to convey their ideas.

1 What technical skills do children require?

They include the ability to:
- maintain good **posture** and **alignment**
- move with **flexibility** to include twisting, stretching and bending
- develop **strength**
- sustain **balance**, control and body tension
- **contract** and **extend** the spine
- **isolate** individual body parts
- **co-ordinate** movements and body parts
- **link** steps, gestures and phrases fluently
- demonstrate a sense of performance through **focus, extension** and **projection**
- dance with **feeling** and **artistry**
- perform with clarity of **style** and **expression**

The above skills will enable children to:
- perform with **accuracy of action**, (travel, jump, turn, gesture, stillness, transference of weight)
- perform movement **rhythmically** with **accuracy** of **dynamic** qualities (time, weight, space and flow)
- perform with **accuracy** in **space** (level, direction, pathway, body shape)

The above elements may be taught within simple set studies, and may include
- **Technical routines**, e.g. a travelling and turning sequence
- **Folk dance**, e.g. Circassian circle
- **Social dance**, e.g. rock and roll

Technique should be taught as a *means* to an *end* and not an end in itself. Children should constantly be made aware of the expressive qualities of movement throughout the acquisition of performing skills.

2 *What performing skills do children require?*

These can be grouped under the following headings:

▌ What the body can do – **action**
   ▌ How the body moves – **dynamics**
      ▌ Where the body moves – **space**

▌ Action

There are six basic body
actions:

- **Travel**
  walking, skipping,
  running, galloping, polkas,
  chassés, travelling on other
  body parts

- **Turn**
  part or whole turns,
  turning using different
  body parts and levels,
  twisting and spiralling

- **Transference of weight**
  moving from one part of
  the body to another – e.g.
  rocking and arching

- **Stillness**
  a pause in movement
  e.g. balance

- **Gesture**
  movement of a part of the
  body which is not bearing
  any weight – e.g. head,
  shoulders, arms, hands,
  spine, hips, legs, feet

- **Jump**
  one foot to the other foot
  – a leap
  one foot to the same foot
  – a hop
  one foot to two feet
  two feet to two feet
  two feet to one foot

Some of these actions may be performed:
   by the **whole** body
   by **parts** of the body
   by a part leading the movement, stressing the body part, or
   by stressing the body **surface**, e.g. palms of hands,
   fingertips

Words related to body actions – whole body or body parts

step	hop	skip	whirl	pounce	balance
leap	circle	dash	arch	bounce	tremble
slide	rock	strike	lift	shoot	sway
swing	shake	punch	swirl	wiggle	lash
toss	rise	stretch	lunge	dip	fall
dive	turn	shrug	twirl	gallop	dodge
push	spiral	hover	melt	whip	chop

▌ Dynamics

There are four elements of movement which highlight its expressive characteristics. They give dance its 'colour' and provide the *dynamics* which movement requires to make it expressive. Everyday actions and gestures form the basic vocabulary of dance. It is *how* these are performed that transforms their meaning into something significant.

- **Time** – Sudden (Quick) ⟷ Sustained (Slow, Smooth)
- **Weight** – Strong (Heavy) ⟷ Light (Gentle)
- **Space** – Direct (Straight) ⟷ Indirect (Curved)
- **Flow** – Free (Difficult to stop movement) ⟷ Bound (Moving with restraint and control)

These elements should be combined in a variety of ways to extend the expressive potential of movement, e.g.

- in a dance using the movements of fire as a stimulus;
  the actions could stress *quick, light, indirect* movements to symbolise the flickering flames;
  the use of *slow, light, indirect* movements would convey a floating quality, appropriate for a dreamlike mood or movement of smoke.

The same movement may suggest a range of meanings, be used in a variety of dance styles and serve different purposes depending on *how* it is performed, e.g.

- in a happy dance walking steps could be performed in a *quick, light* and *bouncy* style, with little emphasis on restraint, to convey the joyfulness of the mood;
  in a sad dance walking steps could be performed in a *slow, strong, direct* manner, perhaps with a feeling of control, to suggest sorrow and inner grief.

- an opening arm gesture may be performed with the emphasis on *slow, direct* and *strong* movement qualities; this could be used to convey a feeling of power, authority and magnificence;
  the identical gesture performed using *slow, direct* and *light* movement qualities might suggest peace, calm and welcome.

Words related to the dynamic features of dance

explode	jab	firm	whip	direct
pounce	flexible	zip	smooth	strong
disjointed	crumble	continuous	bouncy	bendy
dart	legato	dash	relaxed	staccato
glide	light	drift	float	flutter

▎Space

- **Directions**   i.e. up and down (rising and falling), side to side (opening and closing), forwards and backwards (advancing and retreating), diagonally from corner to corner

- **Pathways**   in the air or on the floor, i.e. straight or curved patterns

- **Levels**   i.e. high
  medium
  low

- **Size**   large   ⟷   small
  far   ⟷   near
  opening   ⟷   closing
  (extending)   (contracting)

- **Body shape**   in space, e.g. curved, twisted, angular, wide, narrow

Words related to the spatial features of dance

surround	repel	explore	fill	shrink	sideways
contract	extend	above	beside	below	stretch into
stretch away from	clockwise	anti-clockwise	reverse	symmetric	asymmetric
diagonal	direct	wide	arrow-like	narrow	round

CREATING OR COMPOSING *dances*

Children need to acquire knowledge and understanding of how to create, structure and form their movement ideas. The teaching and development of compositional skills is essential to enable children to create dances which have the potential to communicate meaning.

1 What are the processes children use to compose dances?

These include the ability to:

▮ **explore** and **improvise** movement in response to a stimulus e.g. The Silent Movies (see page 119).

▮ **select** appropriate movement content to express the idea(s) e.g. the villain uses enlarged gestures, holds threatening body shapes and travels in a strong and forceful manner.

▮ **create** a simple phrase or **motif** of movement e.g. a motif containing travel, gesture and stillness which is appropriate to characterise the villain

▮ **develop** the phrases or motifs with the use of repetition, variation and contrast in body actions, spatial aspects and dynamic qualities e.g. the motif could be repeated travelling in different directions; a turn could be introduced into the motif.

2 What are the compositional features which give the dance its form?

▮ motif development
▮ variation
▮ repetition
▮ contrast

▮ start, middle and end
▮ highlights
▮ transitions
▮ harmony

▮ unity
▮ proportion and balance
▮ sequence

Overall Form and Structure of the Dance

Each dance should have a clear beginning, middle and ending. It may be appropriate to use simple guiding structures such as those found in music composition, e.g.

Binary (AB)   – 'A' section, followed by a different 'B' section.

Ternary (A B A)   – 'A' section, 'B' section, repeat of the 'A' section

Rondo or Chorus and Verse (A B A C A D) – 'A' section is the chorus that is repeated after each different verse

3   *What elements guide group choreography?*

▌ Copying

when both partners do the same as each other; the shape, level, quality, rhythm, body part may be copied

▌ Mirroring

when both partners reflect each other's movement exactly in a mirror image, e.g. when one dancer moves her left foot, the other dancer will move her right foot

▌ Complementing

when the shape and movements of one dancer are balanced by the shape and movements of the other, e.g. both dancers do the same basic curved movement as each other but one dancer adapts her movement slightly, perhaps by altering the level or direction

▌ Unison

when the group perform the movement at the same time as each other

▌ Question and answer

when dancers have a conversation using movement

▌ Canon

when one or more movements are danced after each other by the group, e.g. a phrase may be repeated several times by each dancer. Dancer A starts, Dancer B joins in after A has completed one phrase. Dancer C joins in when Dancer B has completed one phrase, etc.

▌ Action and reaction

when one dancer moves while the other dancer keeps still e.g. one dancer may use strong, sudden gestures; the other dancer may reply by using lighter, sustained gestures

4 What relationship can the dancer have to another person(s) or an object – with whom or what does the body move?

▌ **Solo**
a dancer may dance on their own, or as an individual in a group

▌ **Trio**
using three dancers

▌ **Duet**
a dance for two people; this may involve meeting and parting; leading and following; dancing together or apart; taking it in turns to dance

▌ **Small/large group**
involving four or more dancers in a variety of different relationships e.g. **huddles**

▌ **Object or prop**
e.g. chair, cane, hat, ribbon

```
    *   *
*   *   *
```

```
              *
         *   *
    *   *         *   *   *
    *
```

lines
```
*   *   *   *
  *   *   *

*   *   *   *
  *   *   *
```

circles
```
        *
    *         *
      *  *
    *        *
  *        *
    *     *
      * *
    *        *
        *
```

solid group formations
```
*  *  *  *  *  *
  *  *  *  *  *
    *  *  *  *
      *  *  *
        *  *
          *
```

```
          *
        *   *
      *   *   *
    *   *   *   *
  *   *   *   *   *
*   *   *   *   *   *
```

scattered
```
        *        *
            *
    *       *
  *              *       *
```

VIEWING *dance*

Viewing dance, both during the creative process and of the final product is an integral aspect of children's dance appreciation. Although in the past, this area of dance education has frequently been neglected, its importance has now been recognised.

▌ Children need to be aware that dance is a **medium for expression** and **communication.** It is through regular observation and discussion of professional work and classroom work that they learn to appreciate the language of dance, coming to know and understand the art.

▌ Aesthetic appreciation needs to focus on three major inter-related areas:

sensory qualities

expressive qualities

formal qualities

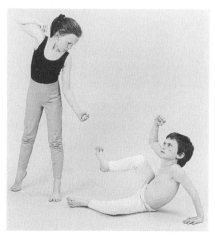

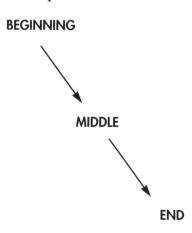

the intrinsic features of the movement, shape, line, pattern

the feelings and meanings conveyed by the movement

the structure and form of the dance related to composition, choreographic designs used and construction devices

What viewing skills do children require?

They include the ability to:
▌ look and listen perceptively and with imagination
▌ interpret and evaluate through attending to the following specific features of the work.

▌ **The Dance Idea:**

● was the initial idea a suitable subject/stimulus for a dance?
● did it evoke an emotional response and arouse the senses?
i.e. did the audience feel sad or excited; did they become involved in the meaning of the dance?

▌ **The Music or Accompaniment:**

Was it
● suitable for the idea?
● complementary to the movement?
● used in its entirety or cut without care?
● of an appropriate rhythmic structure?

The Form:

- were the motifs clear and the basis of the dance?
e.g. were they re-stated imaginatively, suitably sequenced, and combined in various ways?
- was repetition used sensitively?
- were the original movements varied and developed?
- were contrast and highlights used to enrich the meaning?
- was there a sense of proportion and balance between the sections of the dance?
- did it include appropriate choreographic elements?
e.g. canon, action and reaction or mirroring

The Complete Dance:

- was it significant and worth watching?
- was it interesting and relevant throughout?
- was there enough depth and variety in the material content or was it too simple and predictable?
- was the style of the dance clearly established and maintained throughout?
- was the choice of music, or other accompaniment, appropriate?

The Movement Content:

- was it relevant and varied, or merely stereotypical?
- did it convey meaning?
- was there a variety of action content?
- was the full dynamic range of movement explored?
- was the dance visually interesting with a variety of lines and shapes in space?
- were a range of patterns and designs created by the group relationships?

The Performance:

- was it danced with technical accomplishment?
- was it expressive and artistic?
- did it enrich the dance?
- was the interpretation appropriate to the choreographer's intention?

Staging/Design:

- was the decor relevant to the idea?
- were the costumes of a suitable colour and style?
- did the lighting, props, etc. detract from or enhance the dance?

It should always be recognised that the scope of each child's critical appreciation of dance will be determined by their previous knowledge and experience of and in dance. Appreciation is not just static acceptance or an adulatory response, nor is it the use of prescriptive criteria which may result in destructive criticism. Children should be encouraged to engage in imaginative and critical involvement with dance if they are to develop artistic understanding and aesthetic sensitivity.

SECTION THREE

The Teaching of Dance

introduction

The principles for developing a dance curriculum are the same as for any other subject. The content of the programme is to a large extent determined by the National Curriculum which identifies statutory requirements in the form of Attainment Targets, End of Key Stage Statements and Programmes of Study. These are designed to provide teachers with a supportive curriculum framework to aid the planning, delivery and assessment of specific subject areas.

The Programme of Study for Dance within the National Curriculum for Physical Education indicates the appropriate knowledge and skills to be taught at each Key Stage. It effectively constitutes a dance syllabus and provides clear directional guidance for the development of a more detailed Scheme of Work.

The following dance syllabus reflects the National Curriculum Programme of Study for Dance and is specifically designed to give a progressive and developmental framework for the interrelated teaching of Dance Performance, Composition and Appreciation.

A DANCE PROGRAMME OF *Study/syllabus*

Children should, individually, with a partner and in small groups:

KEY STAGE 1

Stimulus

▌ experience working with a range of contrasting stimuli, particularly music and language.
e.g. the use of words, poetry and stories to stimulate imaginative movement responses.

Performing

▌ experience and develop control, co-ordination, balance and poise in basic bodily actions including travelling, jumping, turning, gesturing and stillness, and in isolated use of body parts.
e.g. running and holding a clear body shape, showing an awareness of extension or contraction.

▌ work on contrasts of speed, tension, continuity, shape, size, direction and level, exploring their expressive qualities.
e.g. quick, light skips in a happy dance, strong stamping steps in an angry dance.

Composing

▌ be given opportunities to explore moods and feelings through improvisation and structured tasks.
e.g. exploring movements which convey feeling lost and frightened, selecting tentative, small gestures and steps.

▌ be helped to develop rhythmic responses and clear phrases of movement.
e.g. clapping and walking to the beat of the music,
performing simple folk dances from various countries.

▌ experience and be guided towards making dances with clear beginnings, middles and ends.
e.g. a clown dance which starts with funny runs and walks, includes a section showing balancing tricks with a partner and ends with the whole class dancing in a circle.

Viewing

▌ be given opportunities to observe and describe dance movements and be guided towards identifying their expressive features.
e.g. notice whether the movements are smooth or bouncy; identifying the difference between leaping and hopping actions.

KEY STAGE 2

Stimulus

▮ experience working with a range of stimuli which may incorporate work from other areas of the curriculum, particularly the performing arts and humanities.
e.g. exploring issues related to conservation and the environment through dance, such as whale hunting and the destruction of rain forests.

Performing

▮ be given opportunities to increase the range and complexity of body actions and use of body parts, exploring different dance styles.
e.g. a sequence involving swift runs, and turning into a held, high balanced position.

▮ be guided to perform movements expressively by varying their dynamic and spatial qualities.
e.g. a warrior dance using high powerful leaps and strong angular gestures.

Composing

▮ be given opportunities to express ideas and feelings through improvised and structured tasks, involving exploring, selecting and refining the movement content.
e.g. exploring movements appropriate for a 'carnival' dance and selecting suitable lively travelling steps and gestures.

▮ rhythmically structure and form movement into phrases, creating dances which involve simple development of movement content, contrast and repetition.
e.g. with a partner, one happy and one sad copying and contrasting each other's movement.

Viewing

▮ be guided to develop interpretative as well as descriptive language when appraising dance, their own and that of others.
e.g. associating the dancer shaking his fists with the expression of conflict.

KEY STAGE 3

Stimulus

▌ be given opportunities to independently explore their own ideas and those of others.
e.g. suggest their own poetry/prose to provide the stimulus for creating a duet expressing peace and harmony.

Performing

▌ be guided to perform short dances set by the teacher or their own dance studies, showing an understanding of technique and style.
e.g. perform a range of isolated body actions to a piece of jazz music.

▌ develop and use appropriate dance styles and techniques to communicate meanings and ideas.
e.g. strong, dramatic actions with sudden changes of direction used in a 'gang warfare' dance.

Composing

▌ be guided to create dances whose form includes motifs, development and variation of movement content, repetition and transitions.
e.g. using the accompaniment of an African drum rhythm to create a travelling phrase which may be developed through adding jumps and turns; perform it in unison and canon with a partner.

Viewing

▌ be guided to describe, analyse and interpret dances recognising their main stylistic differences, aspects of production and cultural/historical contexts.
e.g. watching a video of professional dance and describing the features of the style, commenting upon the appropriateness of the movement content and whether it successfully communicates its ideas to the audience.

Presentation and Production

▌ be given opportunities to research and use resource material to support their learning in dance, and to record dance in words and symbols.
e.g. select suitable pictures showing professional dance from which to create a travelling movement phrase and draw its floor pattern.

KEY STAGE 4

Performing

▌ perform complex and technically more demanding dances accurately and expressively.
e.g. dance a set sequence in a contemporary style with an awareness of focus and projection.

▌ be given opportunities to dance in a range of styles which successfully communicate the artistic intention.
e.g. dance to the accompaniment of 'Blues' music conveying the mood of the piece.

Composing

▌ be given opportunities to create dances showing an understanding of form and content, and their expressive significance.
e.g. create a dance concerned with racial prejudice using repetition and development of specific gestures, performed in unison and in canon by the group, and based upon a chorus and verse structure.

Viewing

▌ be guided to discern and critically appreciate all aspects of dance – choreography, performance, context and production.
e.g. interpret a range of meanings and influence of the cultural context on a dance created for worship.

Presentation and Production

▌ be guided to design aspects of production for their own choreography and enabled to record dance.
e.g. stage a duet using suitable lighting and costumes.

GUIDELINES FOR THE DEVELOPMENT OF A SCHEME OF *Work for dance*

Like all other subject areas, a dance scheme of work needs to contain a more detailed analysis of the areas of knowledge, skills and understanding to be developed at each Key Stage of the dance programme or syllabus.

An effective scheme of work will cover *all* or *most* of the following information:

▌ Rationale for dance

This is a statement which explains *why* dance is included in the curriculum and *what* its special contribution is to a child's education (see page 14). It should reflect the curriculum aims and ethos of the school.

▌ Objectives

The objectives and learning outcomes need to relate to the dance programme of study or syllabus and state the specific aspects of Dance Performance, Composition and Appreciation to be taught within a unit(s), module(s) or series of lessons at each Key Stage. They must make direct reference to the teaching and learning to take place and include:

- the knowledge, concepts, skills, values and attitudes to be acquired
- the processes through which these will be achieved and developed
- continuity and progression within the Key Stage and from one to the next.

The objectives should provide a tool for assessment.

▌ Content

This will contain specific reference to the performing skills, compositional features, choreographic elements and aspects of appreciation to be taught within the unit(s), module(s) or lessons.

▌ Teaching and Learning Styles

The teaching and learning styles need to meet the requirements described in the objectives. A range of appropriate methods including resource-based teaching and learning may be evident for:

- the different types of activities and tasks
- children with different needs and abilities.

▌ Resources

The resources needed will depend on *what* is to be delivered and *how*. Different teaching and learning styles will demand different uses of resources. The scheme of work will need to list:

- what resources are available
- how they might be used
- where they are
- how they can be obtained
- rules for their use where appropriate.

In individual, units, modules, or lesson(s) specific reference will need to be made to the *stimuli* and *music* to be used.

▌ Cross-curricular Links

Dance is a tremendous medium for exploring cross-curricular issues and aspects of learning in *all* subject areas. It is important to refer to these links within the scheme of work or selected elements contained in units, modules or lessons.

Assessment and Evaluation Strategies

Assessment is an integral part of the teaching and learning process and should link to the learning outcome(s). It enables pupils to demonstrate in a variety of ways what they *understand* and *can* do! The scheme of work should identify the appropriate assessment techniques and processes both formative and summative with indications of how they will be used, recorded and reported.

Evaluation

The scheme of work is a practical working document which may be reviewed and changed when and if appropriate. There should be a statement in the scheme which describes how the evaluation will take place.

Please note – Assessment and Evaluation Strategies in Dance should reflect a Whole School Policy for these vital processes intrinsic to effective teaching and learning.

And finally, successful schemes of work have the following common features:

■ they are devised by 'teams' of teachers who feel they have *ownership* of the scheme

■ they are regularly discussed and reviewed

■ they are easily communicated to others, including teaching colleagues, governors, parents and children

■ they describe *what* is delivered in the classroom by the individual teacher

■ they *involve* the *children* in the planning process!

ASSESSMENT IN *dance*

Assessment is at the *heart* of the process of promoting children's learning.

As teachers we are continually engaged in assessment of different kinds: analysis, interpretation, judgement, appraisal, evaluation, appreciation and marking. High-quality learning is dependent on the high-quality execution of these processes. This requires high-quality teachers who possess the appropriate cognitive repertoire for a subject to enable them to make skilled interventions within the teaching and learning process. This is the fundamental essence of a teacher's professional responsibility.

The importance of the interrelationship between teaching, learning and assessment cannot be overemphasised. As the skilled intervener within the dynamic partnership between teacher and child, the teacher must be involved in the following types of assessment relating to children's work, in order to promote high-quality learning.

Formative:	to ensure that ongoing achievements are recognised, directional feedback is given, and the next stages in learning are planned.
Summative:	to record the overall achievement and progress of a child in a systematic and meaningful way which will accurately inform other teachers, parents, and most importantly, the child concerned.
Diagnostic:	to scrutinise areas of learning difficulty and high achievement in order to provide the appropriate support and guidance.
Evaluative:	to provide a systematic procedure for curriculum review and to acknowledge, achievements and development targets.

Principles for assessment in dance

▮ Assessment in dance and all the arts should form a natural part of teaching and learning activities.

▮ Assessment activity should arise from current classroom practice.

▮ Assessment should build upon a child's previous experience.

▮ Assessment should relate to the learning outcomes identified in the objectives or specific tasks set within the classroom.

▮ Assessment should match the child's abilities.

▮ Assessment should be a shared process with the child, she/he needs to know *what* is expected and *why* their learning environment has been structured in specific ways.

▮ Assessment should *involve* the child who should be challenged to reflect critically on her/his learning in terms of the *process* involved and the *product* achieved.

▮ Assessment should focus on whether the learning outcome(s) matched the curricular intention(s).

Methods of dance assessment

Through *verbal*, *visual* and *auditory* means a teacher engages in the different processes of assessment in order to collect the appropriate information. This will enable them to make the informed and critical judgements necessary to guide the skilled intervention and interaction between teacher and child.

Throughout the teaching and learning process the teacher will be actively employing one or more of the following methods for the collection of this information:

▮ **talking** to children individually or in groups as they are creating their dances or reflecting on their products.

▮ **listening** carefully to what children say as they discuss the dance challenges set or as they appreciate their own work or the work of others.

▮ **observing** children throughout the creative process and during the performance and presentation of their dances.

▮ **looking** at a video of the children composing and performing their dances.

▮ **analysing** written work in children's personal diaries, the class log book, or written notes, diagrams and records of their dances.

▮ **reflecting** on relevant information contained in the children's profiles and records.

Guiding questions for the teacher during the planning phase

▌ Is there a clear purpose for the dance unit, module or lesson? Does it relate to the dance programme of study?

▌ Are the objectives clearly identified in terms of Performance, Composition and Appreciation?

▌ Have cross-curricular links been fully explored? How will reference be made to the conceptual links in the arts, in particular with music and drama? For example, the development of a musical phrase and dance motif using repetition, or the use of gesture in dance and drama.

▌ Are affective qualities encouraged within aspects of artistic learning related to creating and performing dance? For example, tenacity and perseverance in the selection of appropriate movements to convey meaning.

▌ How will the appropriate expression of feeling be appraised within the process and product? This is vital if the unique educational value of dance and the arts is to be recognised and understood by the children.

▌ Have the children been involved in the planning process of the particular unit, module or lesson? Are they encouraged to build upon previous learning experiences?

▌ Do the dance tasks and challenges fulfil the intended outcomes?

▌ Is there evidence of differentiation and appropriate use of teaching and learning styles?

▌ Are the resources clearly labelled, accessible and organised?

Guiding questions for the teacher during and after the teaching phase

▌ How did the children respond and participate in the individual/group tasks set?

▌ Did the groups display sensitivity, empathy, consideration for each other?

▌ Was there evidence of critical reflection?

▌ Were they challenged?

▌ Did the dance tasks set, allow children to learn independently? Were they appropriately designed and differentiated to develop previous skills and knowledge related to performance, composition and appreciation?

▌ Was sufficient time allowed for the children to reflect on their dance products, to make refinements and adjustments and to rehearse before presentation?

▌ Were observation and discussion opportunities created for the children to engage in artistic and aesthetic appreciation of their work?

▌ Were the questions designed to focus on elements of performance, composition and appreciation to aid the interpretation and meaning of dance?

▌ Was there a focus for the development of their perceptual skills relating to the sensory, expressive and formal qualities of the dance?

▌ Were motifs and dance phrases *appropriately* selected to give form to their feelings and ideas?

▌ Did the learning outcomes match the intentions?

▌ Were the children willing to take risks, imitate, share, respond with imagination and feeling during the artistic process?

▌ How did the children assess and record their dances, both in the making and in the performing?

PLANNING AND TEACHING A *dance lesson(s)*

The following guide will aid the planning and teaching process prior to and during the lesson.

Before the lesson: the planning phase
Stage One

Decide on the starting point – where to begin?
- Select the **idea** for the dance.
- **Decide** on the **nature** of the **stimulus**. This may be one or more of the following types:

Auditory:	music, sounds, words, percussion, poems, stories
Visual:	pictures, designs, sculptures, objects
Tactile:	props, objects
Ideational:	ideas which generate movement that tells a story or communicates
Kinaesthetic:	movement used as a starting point for dance

Ensure a variety of **stimuli** are presented throughout a series of lessons to inspire imaginative, creative responses from the children.

- **Brainstorm** the stimulus for dance ideas and, select an appropriate accompaniment.

Ideas Associated with the Stimulus

Trainers   Ballet shoes

Wellington boots   Flippers

Tapshoes   **Stimulus**   Clogs

Greek sandals   SHOES   High-heels

Music/Accompaniment
Appropriate rhythmic
accompaniment

Age: Nursery/Reception
- **Select** appropriate music/accompaniment and decide on the type of dance, e.g. comic, narrative, abstract, dramatic, social, folk etc.

Style of Dance
Dramatic or
Narrative

- **Decide** if any additional resources are required e.g. prop, poem, painting, object.

Stage Two

Consider ways of developing aspects of the stimulus into a suitable Dance Framework – how to structure ideas into a simple dance form?

▌ Select appropriate ideas from the brainstorm and translate them into possible **performing skills, compositional** features and **choreographic elements.** Highlight the main focus in these three areas. (See pages 19–25)

Possibilities for Movement Exploration

PERFORMING SKILLS		COMPOSITION

▌ Stepping and jumping with an awareness of strong body tension.
▌ Use of curving and straight floor patterns.

Stimulus
WELLINGTON BOOTS

▌ Copy/follow my leader.
▌ Repetition of stamping phrase.

Stage Three

▌ **Plan the dance framework.** This provides the structure and the overall **form** of the dance as anticipated by the teacher and the children. It may be relatively simple or complex. It provides material for one or a series of lessons as exemplified in the dance modules. Listen to the accompaniment to help you structure the dance framework. This needs to contain:

- The **start** of the dance, how it **develops** and **concludes.**
- Whether it is an **individual, partner** or **group** dance within a series of dances.
- The specific **movement content** focus for each section and how this might develop. This will inform the exploration for the dance and guide the movement tasks designed by the teacher and the children during the lesson(s).
- The **compositional** features to be developed and the **choreographic elements** involved. If using music, the form of the piece will guide you. Listen for repetitions, contrasts and simple developments of content.

A Sample Dance Framework –
Composing the Movement

▌ Start in a clear statue shape to show off the boots.
▌ Stamping phrase on the spot to a simple rhythm – repeat.
▌ Marching steps following the class teacher – include changes of direction.
▌ Individually create a hopping and leaping phrase across wet puddles on the floor.
▌ Finish – stuck in the mud. Tug of war with boots to create own ending.

The children may dance with their boots on or off, having explored ways of travelling while wearing them.

Stage Four

Design appropriate movement tasks to complement and achieve the Dance Framework

▌ Ensure the **starting activities** are varied and suitable for the dance lesson. These may include travelling steps, movement of isolated body parts, swinging actions, curling and extending the spine, stretching, turning and jumping. (See pages 47–56).

▌ Decide on the main **performing skills** to be developed in each phase of the dance framework.

▌ Design movement tasks which enable the children to **explore, select** and **refine** appropriate motifs.

▌ **Compositional** features should be an integral aspect of the movement tasks, together with opportunities for dance **appreciation** and **observation** (See pages 26–7).

It may be necessary to adapt and adjust the movement tasks planned in response to the children's needs. However, it is always important to have a clear idea how you would like the dance to be developed – this gives you confidence!

During the lesson: the teaching phase
Stage One

Starting Activities and Introduction to the Stimulus

For starting activities please refer to the guidance notes on page 47.

Aims:

▌ To stimulate children's imagination and provoke creative responses;

▌ To explore the use of a variety of stimuli to enhance the dance potential of the chosen idea;

▌ To integrate dance ideas with Topic/Thematic work, if appropriate, so that the children perceive the holistic nature of their learning experiences.

Content:

▌ Select a **variety** of relevant **stimuli** to elicit creative and imaginative responses from the children;

▌ Use **professional videos** if available, and children's work if appropriate;

▌ Encourage the children to bring their own **stimuli** for dance;

▌ Draw on the powerful use of **language** to convey the 'expressive' qualities of the stimulus.

Aspects to consider:

▌ Plan to use '**carpet time**' in the classroom to prepare for the dance lesson.

▌ **Gather** the children around you for **discussion**, make sure their eyes are on you or the resources.

▌ **Listen to the accompaniment** as a group – before the lesson if possible. Encourage the children to clap, stamp their feet, snap their fingers to the beat.

▌ Use **open-ended questioning** techniques, e.g. How did the music make you feel? Suggest a way of travelling to the music. Will your steps be strong or light?

▌ Discuss the **expressive qualities**, the compositional structures and the form of the music with the children.

▌ Encourage **listening** skills.

▌ **Avoid lengthy discussions** to ensure the children concentrate and remain warm.

▌ Allow the children to **discuss** their ideas in two's.

Stage Two

Exploration of the Stimulus, Movement Content and Technical Skills to be developed

Aim:
To explore and structure movement ideas into the dance form as outlined in the dance framework.

Content:
▌ Select the appropriate **body actions, qualities** and **spatial** aspects to be considered, for each part of the dance. What? How? Where? (see pages 20–22)

▌ Select the **choreographic** elements to be employed; (see pages 24–5)

▌ Decide on the **compositional** features to be developed; (see page 23)

▌ Consider the appropriate times to encourage **dance appreciation** through observation during all phases of the lesson.

The following guide provides a focus to *aid* the *design* of *movement tasks*:

1 Exploration of Movement Ideas

This may be teacher **directed**, teacher **guided** or **improvisation**.

Aspects to consider:
▌ Do not be afraid to provide a **simple structure** to aid this process. Young children need security to build up their confidence. They cannot create in a vacuum!

▌ Be clear about the **focus** for **technical development**. This should complement lesson objectives.

▌ It is important to design tasks along a continuum from closely structured to more open-ended challenges. This will depend on the:

- **experience** of the children;
- **content** selected, whether it is new or familiar;
- **stage of development** within the unit of work;
- the children's **response** to the chosen stimulus.

During a lesson or series of lessons the tasks may move from closed ←→ open

2 Selection of Movement Ideas to Form a Motif

Having explored the movement ideas children should be encouraged to select appropriate ideas to form a **motif**. This should:

- contain a clear **starting** and **finishing** position with fluid transitions;
- begin to **communicate the idea** and have meaning;
- be capable of **repetition**;
- possess movement material with the **potential for development**.

Aspects to consider:

▮ Ensure you are **familiar** with the music or accompaniment and know its structure – this will help the children to form their ideas.

▮ **Record** the music several times to avoid rewinding the tape.

3 Development of the Motif

▮ With very young children the dance may be one simple phrase. As they develop technical expertise and compositional knowledge they will be capable of performing more complex dances.

▮ Development ideas will include:

- **adding** one movement to the original movement;
- **extending** the motif by more than one movement;
- **repeating** the motif;
- **creating** another motif – this may be a contrasting one;
- **enlarging** the movement content;
- **varying** the dynamic, spatial qualities, actions and relationships;
- **re-organising** the content of the motif.

▮ Listen to the music to guide you!

Aspects to consider:

▮ Encourage children to learn **each other's** motifs – this improves their technical ability and their observational skills.

▮ Ensure instructions are **clear**. How many movements? How long? When to start? When to finish? Children need guidance – do not be afraid to be prescriptive within an open task.

▮ Encourage children to **concentrate** on the selected technical aspects – demand the highest quality that they are capable of.

▮ Stress the '**expressive**' aspects of the movement.

▮ Give the children an opportunity to **refine** motifs before performing and observing each other – children do *not* enjoy showing work that they are not proud of!

▮ Incorporate a **mental rehearsal** before asking the children to show their work.

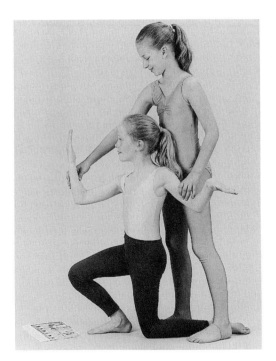

▮ **Teach whole group** motifs to develop specific skills. This may help in the structuring of the dance and give it unity and coherence.

▮ Employ the use of **choreographic elements** in developing motifs when children are dancing in a duo, trio or in a small group (see page 25).

4 Construction of the Dance

The complexity of this will depend on the **age, experience** and **understanding** of the children. Simple forms are: **AB; ABA; chorus and verse, ABAC** (see page 23).

Aspects to consider:

▌ Use the music selected to **guide** the overall **form**.

▌ With young children several of the following techniques may be employed to structure dance forms:

- a **circle** dance – moving in to the middle and out, across the middle to change places, around the circle;
- a **follow my leader** – dance in pairs or small groups changing the leader;
- a **small group dance** – dancing towards, away from, making a file, circle;
- a **teacher and class dance** – dance near the teacher, follow the teacher, dance away from the teacher, do the same as the teacher;
- a **half class dance** – half the class hold positions, the other half dance, reverse and repeat. Finish with the whole class dancing together.

Stage Three

Performing and Appreciating the Dance
Please refer to the guidance notes on pages 57–8.

At a glance... the lesson structure...
Appreciation and **Observation** should be planned and taught throughout the various stages of the lesson

Starting Activities and Introduction to Stimulus
Common principles apply to body preparation for dance:
(Refer to guidance notes on pages 47–56)

Creating the Dance
Movement Content and Technical Skills
to be developed

Performing and Appreciating the Dance
These are integral aspects of all dance lessons.
(Refer to guidance notes on pages 57–8)

GUIDANCE NOTES
Music for dance

This section was contributed by Sarah Hennessy, Lecturer in Education at the School of Education, University of Exeter.

There is a natural and instinctive relationship between music and dance which is most apparent in the responses of young children. Music might almost be described as the expression of movement in sound. Music has pulse and rhythm which gives it life and energy. When the pulse is slow-moving and the rhythm patterns are regular or even indistinct then the music can make us feel peaceful, calm, thoughtful or relaxed. In contrast a strong beat, employing more complex rhythm patterns creates in us a feeling of excitement or agitation.

Young children, when singing or listening to music will, quite naturally, move rhythmically and expressively. A combination of growing self awareness and lack of opportunity frequently stifles this natural joy of dancing and for most people music becomes an activity divorced from expressive movement. We are trained to stand still in the choir, to use a minimal amount of movement when playing an instrument, and definitely not to tap our feet in the orchestra. But musicians and listeners outside the 'classical' tradition move and dance naturally and appropriately to their music. The more opportunities we have for experiencing music through dance the more sensitive and expressive music makers and listeners we will become, and vice versa.

A piece of music will often be the starting point for dance so it is worth taking some care over choosing and getting to know it. What you choose will be informed by the purpose of the dance. The music might:

▌ provide an unobtrusive background;
▌ accompany starting activities or technical exercises;
▌ set a mood;
▌ provide a framework for a particular dance idea;
▌ suggest a narrative;
▌ accompany a recognised dance style.

Try to avoid very familiar pieces such as 'chart hits' or well-worn dance music. It is difficult to devise fresh ideas when a particular piece has strong associations for you or the children and there is a danger of ending up with something rather predictable or clichéd. Less familiar music should allow everyone to respond in an uncluttered way.

If you use song material consider the lyrics as a source of ideas for the dance. They may tell a story using a direct narrative approach or through imagery and metaphor. The words may suggest a feeling or emotion which should be reflected in the dynamics and movements of the dance.

Having selected your music you and the children need to get to know it. Depending on the circumstances you might find that it can become the material for your music lesson as well. All the listening, analysis and discussion will effortlessly fulfil many of the requirements of your music curriculum and, of course, develop in the children a greater awareness of the musical detail which they can respond to when dancing.

Remember
Dance provides excellent opportunities for composing music. Commission your own or other children (perhaps secondary music students) to compose and record their work for dance. It is often better to tape record the composition as live performance of the music is demanding of players, dancers and the teacher.

Elements to listen for:

Pulse (beat)

Is it heavily emphasised or weak, fast or slow?

▌ In all music the pulse is grouped in some kind of regular way. In most Western music groupings are in 2's, 3's, 4's or 6's though much twentieth-century music can be more adventurous using 5's, 7's or irregular groupings (bars). It is not always easy to hear how the beat is grouped, the simple guide is to listen for the stressed (accented) beat. This is most likely to be the first beat in each bar. For example:

- 1 2, 1 2, 1 2, etc. suggests a marching or walking action. It is also the beat of a polka and a samba;
- 1 2 3, 1 2 3, 1 2 3, etc. is waltz time, minuet time, and gives a rocking, lilting feel;
- 1 2 3 4, 1 2 3 4, etc. is rock and roll time;
- 123456, 123456, etc. which is characterised by a lilting or skipping rhythm as in 'Girls and boys come out to play', 'Humpty Dumpty', jigs and reels.

Remember
The beat continues through silences as well as sound. The speed (tempo) of the music may alter by slowing down, accelerating or changing gear completely.

These are some simple examples and you may need some practice at identifying different timings. Ask your music specialist for reassurance to begin with. You will probably find that there are children in your class who can help. It is not a magic trick and with practice you will find you can do it. The best way, not surprisingly, is to LISTEN and MOVE to the music and you will find that your body will know what to do. If you have the printed music available the time signature will tell you the number of beats in

a bar. This is the pair of numbers printed at the very beginning of the music, one on top of the other; the top number indicates the number of beats in a bar, e.g.

Rhythmic Material

Is it regular, irregular, constant or changing?

▌ The rhythm patterns in folk and 'pop' music are often strong and repetitive. Much late nineteenth- and twentieth-century 'classical' music tends to be much less 'settled' or predictable: the music changes within the composition sometimes very dramatically or unexpectedly.

Melodic Material

Is it flowing, moving by step or 'jumping' about?
Is there a singable tune or are there short repeated motifs?
Are the phrases short or long?

▌ Dramatic leaps in pitch give physical movement to the dance, e.g. Prokofiev's *Romeo and Juliet* ballet – the 'Dance of the Knights'

▌ Think of the shape of the melody, for example, are there regular rises and falls

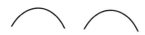

or is it spiky and unpredictable?

Dynamics (Volume)

Are there dramatic or gradual changes?

▌ Dynamics are used to give expression, to vary a repeat (echoes), to signal change or the end, to surprise, to calm, to frighten or to excite. Other elements do this, of course, but not always so obviously.

Texture

Is there one instrument or many?

Is there simple accompaniment of a melody or are these thick layers of sound moving in chords or weaving several different parts together?

▌ A small jazz group will tend to give each instrument an independent 'voice'.

▌ Latin American and many African instrumental styles provide several distinct layers of rhythm played on different percussion instruments.

▌ The symphony orchestra often sounds very dense and complex.

Structure

Is the material repeated a number of times in more or less the same manner or is it varied or transformed?

Are there contrasting sections – how are they organised?

Certain structures are common in many styles of music, e.g.

▌ Ternary – A B A – 'sandwich' where there are two principal themes (or tunes) which contrast with each other (A and B). A is repeated after B providing a kind of symmetry ('Twinkle, twinkle little star' does this).

▌ Binary – two themes A B.

▌ Canon – the theme is heard in different parts or voices, each starting at a different time. Rounds are simple canons.

▌ Rondo – a verse/chorus structure where the 'verse' may be different each time – ABACAD.

The important aspect of musical structure is to become familiar with the way material is repeated or altered and when changes happen.

Silence

Silence is as important as sound. It makes us attend and highlights important moments. It prepares us, it builds tension, provides release and moments of rest.

Remember

Taking a section of music out of a larger work needs careful handling. Give yourself plenty of time to make good quality recordings using the best equipment you can lay your hands on. Adjust the recording level (if this is not automatic) to avoid distortion and, if there is no definite start or finish, fade in and out. Always make a spare copy in case of disaster.

The music chosen for dance needs to have some life of its own. If it is insubstantial, trivial, and unsatisfying on its own it will do nothing to stimulate or enhance the dance ideas. Be adventurous and explore your own collection of recordings in this new light. Listen to the music of other cultures where, often, the relationship between dance and music is much closer. When listening to music from other cultures be aware of the purpose and context given to it within that culture. It may be associated with story telling, work, celebration or religious festivals, and this may influence and help to develop appropriate dance ideas. It is not necessary only to use Chinese music when planning a topic on China. A wide and diverse range of music and songs from different cultures may serve many different purposes in the dance lesson.

In music education, dance:

▌ promotes and develops an understanding of pulse and rhythm;

▌ provides experience and skill acquisition in physical co-ordination;

▌ promotes an awareness of the close relationship between the expressive languages of movement and music;

▌ develops knowledge and understanding of the repertoire through the music composed/and chosen for dance;

▌ provides a stimulus for composition and performance.

STARTING ACTIVITIES FOR *dance*

Aims:

To physically and mentally prepare the children for dance, and to develop their technical skills and knowledge of dance.

Content:

It is important that children learn to prepare their bodies physically to enable them to participate safely and fully in the dance lesson. The teacher will need to engage the children in a range of physical activities which 'warm the body up' by:

▌ *raising* the *heart beat* through simple continuous and repetitive movements, e.g. walks, skips, runs and gallops. This will improve the circulation and result in the children feeling more alive, a little breathless and generally warm throughout the body.

▌ using a variety of exercises which mobilise the joints and improve children's *flexibility* and *suppleness*. These may involve moving individual parts of the body, simple combinations of body parts, e.g. knees and feet, or the whole body, e.g. large swinging actions.

▌ including activities which gradually increase children's *stamina* so that they are able to perform for longer periods of time without becoming short of breath or lacking in body control and co-ordination, e.g. a sequence of jumps, or a combination of travelling steps.

It may be appropriate to invigorate the class initially by asking them to use their hands to rub different parts of their body, e.g. toes, calves, thighs, backs etc., to precede the more vigorous activity. Special attention should be given to preparing children's feet for dancing, ensuring that the muscles and joints are moved gently, particularly in cold weather when dancing on cold floors in bare feet may feel painful.

Aspects to consider:

In every phase of the dance lesson it is important to stress that *how* the children move is essential; that the manner of performance is of central concern to the teacher and the class. This emphasis on the qualitative aspects of movement should originate with the initial warming up activities when good posture, control and extension should be essential features of the children's work. Whilst walking about the dance space children may need to be reminded to 'stand tall', focus on where they are moving, use their feet sensitively to reduce their impact on the floor, and shift their body weight in order to control changes of direction. All movements should be performed with a dance-like quality emphasising dynamics, rhythm, poise and clarity of movement.

This will prove difficult for many children whilst others will display a seemingly natural and easy control of their movements with a feel for the sense of line, shape and fluency necessary in dance. With practice children's ability to dance skilfully and expressively will improve, and the role of the dance teacher is to provide a range of dance experiences which will enable them to develop the necessary physical and technical skills.

A selection taken from the following suggested activities will 'warm the body up'. Both you and the children will be able to add new ideas so that eventually you develop a repertoire of varied and interesting movements. Depending upon the length of your lesson and the dance you are creating, this stage of the work may last between five and ten minutes. Within it you may include specific technical skills which relate to the dance framework, e.g. increasing the time spent on moving isolated body parts in preparation for a 'Machine' dance. You may decide to combine two or three different activities into a sequence, for example, swinging and stretching. However, it is always advisable to repeat the same movements several times, to enable the children to 'feel' them in their own bodies and in an attempt to prepare the body adequately for vigorous movement. Try to include a balance of different activities which develop a range of technical and physical skills,

e.g.	travelling steps swinging and stretching combinations	or	stretching body parts swinging and turning
or	body parts travelling steps floorwork jumps	or	travelling steps stretching body parts combinations

Appropriate music can add to the children's enjoyment and help them to move rhythmically and expressively. It may be necessary to select one or two different pieces to accompany different phases of the 'warm up'.

Common Errors:

Talking too much is a mistake as children learn by moving in dance lessons and it is this action focus that they frequently enjoy most. Aim to involve the children physically and mentally from the outset and talk whilst they are moving, encouraging, praising and guiding their work.

Neglecting to explain to the class why a particular activity will improve their ability to dance, e.g. how stretching the feet when jumping will enhance the quality of their jumps.

Forgetting to praise children whenever possible; learn to perceive small improvements in their work and give them recognition. As children acquire more confidence in the dance lesson the possibilities for developing their creative and imaginative work become far greater. A sense of achievement and personal success will enhance their self esteem and motivate their work in future dance classes.

Things for the children to remember

▮ I am going to work hard. My body is going to get hot and perspire, so I need to change into kit which is suitable.

▮ Wearing jewellery is not safe. I might hurt someone else or myself, so I must remove it.

▮ Loose clothes get in the way. After I have warmed up properly, I need to wear clothing that allows me to move freely, and does not spoil my body shape/line.

▮ *My feet are important!*

Allow the feet to
feel the floor

Improve the quality   Allow the feet to
of movement   BARE FEET   stretch fully

(The floor must be suitable for working in bare feet, otherwise trainers, etc. may be worn.)

I should:

▮ breathe slowly, deeply and evenly;

▮ not stretch to the point where breathing becomes unnatural;

▮ always perform a *non-stretching*, large body movement warm-up to increase body temperature and lubricate joints;

▮ stretch the muscles to be used during the main activity *before* the activity;

▮ hold a stretch in a comfortable position – *Static Stretch* – gradual stretching of a muscle to a position where it is held *without bouncing*; hold the muscle in stretch for ten to twelve seconds;

▮ *never* stretch to a point where there is *pain*. Stretching exercises should be carried out slowly without forcing tight muscles to overstretch. If pain is felt, the muscle should be slightly relaxed until only a feeling of mild tension is felt;

▮ stretch the muscles that have been working during the activity *after* the activity, to help relax the muscle.

Children should be encouraged and guided towards developing their own routine of starting activities. Whenever possible they can start to 'warm their body up' independently based upon their knowledge and understanding of how the body works and principles which apply to safety, e.g. gentle activity should precede more energetic movement, each child needs a safe space to work in. They could work in two's to compose short sequences focusing on, for example, swings, stretches or individual body parts. The whole class might learn some of these sequences and combine them with ideas of their own.

At the end of the lesson incorporate a 'cool down' to enable the children to prepare themselves physically and mentally for the next part of the school day. This might include walking about the space, lying in a relaxed position on the floor, gentle stretches either standing or sitting. The teacher's voice may be useful to alter the mood, give instructions and bring the children from an imaginative situation or role to reality.

Travelling Steps   These will include runs, walks, skips, leaps, hops, gallops, polka and chassé steps.

Suggestions:

1 Walking about the room:

▎ change direction on a given signal, e.g. a change in the music, the sound of a tambour;
▎ follow another person, change to following someone else when you choose;
▎ in two's, place your hand on your partner's back and try to guide them to follow you as you walk about the space.

2 Travelling steps:

– select three different steps and alternate between them;
e.g. skipping, walking and galloping
– perform two different steps, each taking eight counts;
e.g. eight walks, four polka steps
– select two or three travelling steps and repeat them several times, allow a partner to copy them;
– travel making straight or curved floor patterns;
e.g. strong marching steps or swift runs
– run into a balance on the balls of the feet, tip the weight to take you off balance and run in another direction;
– add claps to accompany some of the steps;
– in two's, A claps whilst their partner travels about the room and vice versa;
– whole class copies one child's different steps which are repeated several times.

Remember:
Spatial awareness needs to be emphasised; ensure that the children look for the spaces in the room.
Control of the body in motion; ask the children to change direction, pause or hold a moment of stillness to practise their body control.
Ankle extension; sensitive use of the feet needs to be stressed to promote light footwork.
The rhythm of the different steps may vary, e.g. a skip is a step hop in an uneven rhythm, a polka step is a <u>1</u> and <u>2</u> (♫ ♩) rhythm.

Common Errors:
Allowing children to run *en masse* in a circle around the room.

Lack of clarification between the different steps.

Body Parts or Isolations

This involves moving individual body parts independently from each other and will include circling, shaking, lifting, lowering, turning and stretching specific body parts.

Suggestions:

▌ sitting or kneeling in a space, copy the teacher's use of individual body parts;

▌ in two's copy your partner's use of body parts; take it in turns to lead and follow;

▌ move the body part that is called out by the teacher;

▌ use different sounds/percussion instruments to signify the movement of different body parts, e.g. drums = knees, cabasa = shoulders;

▌ increase the combinations of body parts moving, e.g. hips and shoulders, head and hands, low leg kicks and arm stretches;

▌ use body parts to lead you down to the floor and up towards the ceiling; vary the directions to include the sides, front and back, diagonals;

▌ whole class forms a circle; take it in turns to lead the class, moving individual or combinations of body parts.

Arms:
- stretch high over head,
- reach for the sky one arm after the other (tension)
- let arms drop down and swing gently
- bend arms at the elbows
- 'punch' in various directions

Knees:
- bend and straighten them; have the feet in parallel first/second, and turned out; i.e. plié
- shake and circle them

Head:
- hold head up – long neck, eyes to front
- turn head slowly to left then right
- drop head forwards slowly, then lift up tall
- drop head towards one shoulder and roll it forwards towards the other shoulder

Feet:
- circle each ankle in both directions
- point and flex each foot
- lift the toes off the floor and then the heels
- shake the feet, wriggle the toes
- low, bouncy jumps

Shoulders:
- lift and drop
- circle with arms by sides
- circle with hand on shoulder
- circle with arms up in front and then over the top
- quick shrugging and shaking

Hips:
- move from side to side, circle in both directions
- with knees slightly bent tip the pelvis in each direction, front, side and back.

Back:
- stand with feet slightly apart, knees relaxed, arms bent and in front of body, gently turn at waist to look behind (left to right)
- stand with feet apart, hands on hips, tip to the side (to left and right)
- allow the spine to curve, start with the head and neck, allow the weight of the body to take the torso down towards the floor allowing the knees to bend, as the fingertips touch the floor start to reverse the movement

Hand movements:
- open them wide
- grip them tight
- rotate the wrists
- press palms together and relax (repeat) (feel this movement in the whole body)
- shake them above the head, near the floor, to the side

Remember:
Maintain posture and control of the whole body whilst moving one area.
Stretch the spine without lifting the shoulders; ask the children to shrug their shoulders and then to relax them so that they can feel the difference.
Strong, tight stomachs support the back.
Good posture without exaggerated tension is required.
Each part of the spinal column should be involved when curling the back.

Common Errors:
Involuntary involvement of other parts of the body.
Rigidity in the body rather than extension; use words such as lengthen, elongate, reach, grow, straighten.

Swings   These will include large movements involving the whole body and smaller movements using parts of the body. The feet may be in *parallel*, in either first or second position or *turned out* in either first or second position. The use of a turned out position will allow for greater flexibility and stability.

Whole body movements:

▌ swinging the body up and down from standing to crouching and from side to side
▌ add a small jump to the swing
▌ allow the swing to take you into a travel or turn
▌ imagine you are skiing down the slopes, allow the armswings to go across the body as you slalom down the course and jump over the bumps
▌ create your own sequence of swinging actions, combining body parts and the whole body
▌ teach a specific sequence, e.g. Circle Exercise:
  ● rolling down spine using weight of head to lead the movement
  ● uncurl to finish standing
  ● scoop into ski position with arm swings
  ● figure of eights with arms stretched, knees bending
  ● arms wrapping around waist, knees bending

Remember:
The knees should stay over the toes, whether in parallel or turned out position.
Lengthen the back, lift the arms high.
Allow the weight of the body or body part to give impetus to the swing.

Common Errors:
Lack of control and balance to co-ordinate the swings.
Knees turning inwards.

Stretching   This should involve the whole body and parts of the body, emphasising the torso as the centre of the movement. This will include *standing*, working on pliés and rises onto the toes, stretching the leg muscles, reaching in all directions (side, up, down and back). *Floorwork* includes stretching and flexing the feet, stretching the hamstrings at the back of the legs, twisting the spine, falling and rolling movements.

Suggestions:
▌ bend the knees (pliés) with feet in first and second positions, either in parallel or turned out; combine pliés with rises onto the balls of the feet;
▌ staying in your own place in the room, stretch out to reach as many different points in the space as possible;
▌ after stretching out to a point in space, contract in towards the centre of the body in preparation for another extension;
▌ include different levels, add a roll on the floor;
▌ allow different body parts to initiate and lead the stretch;
▌ vary the dynamics of the movement.

Floorwork   By working on the floor children have fewer problems with maintaining their balance and are provided with support for their movements. They should be encouraged to 'sit on top of the floor' and not collapse into it, stressing the need for body tension and control. ·

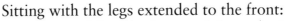

Sitting with the legs extended to the front:
▌ stretch and flex the feet, with legs together or in second position;
▌ start with the arms up above the head, bring them down, slide them along the legs and try to push the toes away, with the legs together or in second position;
▌ with the legs together gently stretch forward from the waist, reach as far as possible and hold the position for at least five seconds;
▌ tuck the knees to the chest and curve the spine over, open out, lift the arms and stretch the legs and toes.

Kneeling:
▌ roll from kneeling onto the bottom and back up to the knees;
▌ hug the knees and rock on to the back and up again.

Common Errors
Becoming tense and shortening the muscles rather than extending and stretching them. Moving in a jerky, sudden manner.

Remember:
Hold the stretch positions for several seconds and feel the body tension.
Repeat the movements several times.
Maintain a sense of correct posture and body alignment.

Turning   This involves changing the point of focus and rotating the body. Turns may be performed on the spot, whilst travelling, on the floor or at different levels.

Remember:

The eyes should focus on the direction of the turn, i.e. spotting. The arms, legs and feet will assist the turn, particularly if the idea of opening the body out to initiate the turn and closing it in to complete it can be introduced.

Common Errors:

Losing balance and control due to a lack of focus and body tension.

Jumps   The feeling of flight is exhilarating and defying gravity can be exciting and challenging. Jumps may vary in height and distance and the footwork may be 2/2, 2/1, 1/1, 1/2, 1 to the other 1.

Suggestions:

Without travelling:

▌ four bouncy jumps with the feet together, four jumps with the legs apart; the legs may be in parallel or turned out
▌ three small jumps, one large explosive jump
▌ four hops, four jumps
▌ four jumps, repeat with a quarter or half turn
▌ large jumps using different body shapes in the air, e.g. straight, curved or twisted
▌ compose 'hopscotch' type sequences on the spot or travelling.

Remember:

On take-off and landing bend the knees and stretch the feet.
On landing, stress the order of contact with the floor as toes, ball of the foot, heel.
Land with the knees aligned over the toes.
In flight, hold the shape in the air.

Common Errors:

Jerking the spine in an effort to gain height.
Heels not touching the floor on landing.

Combinations   This will involve combining steps, jumps and turns into travelling phrases of movement. These may vary in *direction*, using diagonals, lines and different floor patterns and include changes of *rhythm*.

Suggestions:

- four walks, four jumps;
- four skips, four claps;
- combine the above; you might turn the jumps a quarter or half turn each;
- three polka steps and three stamps;
- add a turn to the polka steps;
- a series of leaps across the room;
- step leap, step hop;
- swift runs into a balance, tip forward and run on;
- run and jump; vary the take off and landing to include one and two feet; use different body shapes in the air;
- run, jump and roll on landing;
- four walks forward, four walks in a circle to the right;
- gallop across the room facing your partner;
- gallop four with the right leg leading, four with the left leg leading.

Remember:
State which is the starting foot.
Teach the footwork first, and then add gestures, body shapes etc.
Clarify the direction of travel.
Be explicit about the counting and length of the phrase.

Common Errors:
Inability to recognise the individual steps.
Incorrect timing.

There are endless combinations that will provide children with challenging and exciting movement phrases. Ensure that they know which foot to start on and in which direction they are to travel. Add arm and leg gestures to increase the complexity of the movements and vary the rhythm and tempo of the musical accompaniment.

PERFORMING *dance*

Aims:

To provide an opportunity for the children to perform their dances – an integral aspect of dance as a performing art.

To encourage an awareness of a sense of audience, staging and theatre.

Content:

The final dance may be:
- a simple **motif;**
- a small **part** of the overall dance form;
- **half** the dance;
- the **whole** dance.

Children can perform their dances to:
- the teacher;
- a partner;
- a small group;
- half the class;
- the whole class;
- an invited guest;
- another class;
- an assembly;
- parents, governors;
- the public.

A video of children's work during the process of creating and performing dance can act as a powerful aid and stimulus for individual, technical development.

Performing dance is *not* confined to the end product. Children should be encouraged to refine and present their work **throughout** the lesson or series of lessons.

Aspects to consider:

- Work must be **practised**, **refined** and **rehearsed** to ensure the children can remember the dance.
- Presentation of dance requires **thought** to ensure it is seen to its **best advantage.** Spacing the children and encouraging a sense of **stage front** is important.
- Children need to be constantly reminded that dance is a **performing art** where **communication** and **expression** are intrinsic features. Projection, focus, expression, poise, stage presence are skills to be constantly developed.
- It may be appropriate to **ask** children if they would like to share their work by performing it – some may need time to develop sufficient confidence.
- Be clear in your own mind **why** you are asking the children to perform.

APPRECIATING *dance*

Aims:

To develop children's knowledge, understanding and aesthetic appreciation of dance as an art form.

To encourage children to view dance critically.

Content:

When viewing dance, opportunities need to be created for children to:

❚ talk, draw and write critically and imaginatively about their own work, that of their peers, and other amateur and professional dancers and choreographers;

❚ develop a critical dance vocabulary, one that goes beyond an initial response, such as 'smashing' or 'boring' and encourages them to give reasons for their evaluation based on certain aspects of the dance, e.g. whether the movement was appropriate for a comic dance; were some sections of the dance too long and repetitive;

❚ appreciate a range of dance styles, including social, folk and theatre dance, and to examine their responses in relation to personal opinions and preferences for certain styles of dance.

Aspects to consider:

The teaching should aim to:

❚ be sensitive and open-minded to encourage children to perceive their own interpretation of dances, and look with a more enquiring eye rather than worrying about right or wrong answers; to see things for themselves.

❚ direct children's attention to specific features of the work, giving a focus for their viewing, e.g. identifying movements which are repeated and recognising how these are then varied and developed; noticing the choreographer's use of stage space and how this is linked to the relationships between the dancers; observing the need for clarity of action to improve the performance. This relates to the sensory, expressive and formal qualities of the dance (see page 26).

❚ enrich their dance vocabulary to include factual descriptions such as bouncy jumps, curved arm lines, and also make use of similes and metaphors, e.g. the movements were 'puppet-like', she performed a sparkling leap or a haunting gesture.

❚ include a range of dance styles and information related to the contextual and cultural features of the dance, e.g. in what era they were composed, if they were part of a musical, from which country they originated. This may involve the use of professional dance or video (see page 62).

WHAT *happens if?*

There is no hall?

▮ Use your own classroom space for selected dance ideas, e.g. divide the class into audience and performers; use the 'carpet area' for small group work whilst the class are engaged in other curriculum activities.

▮ Explore other spaces in and around the school, e.g. a classroom with a partition, open resource areas.

▮ Investigate the outside environment, e.g. grassy areas and playground, weather permitting.

▮ Look for alternative spaces within the vicinity, e.g. village hall, community centre, neighbouring school.

I find it difficult to fit dance into my class timetable?

▮ As dance is a valuable part of children's education and a statutory aspect of the NC, it should be taught.

▮ The cross-curricular potential for dance is tremendous, e.g. explore how dance may be included into a topic; could dance fulfil NC requirements in other subject areas such as listening skills and activities in maths and science?

▮ Look at the contribution of dance to children's affective and cognitive development, e.g. the development of self esteem and confidence to share ideas and work in groups; as a medium for encouraging problem solving, creativity and imagination.

I find it difficult to dance myself and I do not know how to begin?

▮ Enthusiasm, interest and a willingness to learn about dance is more important than technical expertise.

▮ Improve your subject knowledge through, e.g. reading a range of literature; visiting a local school where there is dance expertise; inviting a colleague or advisory teacher to work alongside you; exploring the teaching resources, e.g. video material, dance resource packs, or authority guidelines which are available; visiting dance performances, e.g. school, area, county or professional work; arranging for a dance residency in your school; using the BBC dance radio programmes (see page 71).

▮ Use your children to demonstrate and stimulate dance ideas – involve them in the planning and use their expertise.

▮ Attend a local inservice workshop or course, or a suitable dance class in the community.

▮ Practise dancing for fun; try ideas out at home; involve friends and members of the family.

My class includes physically disabled children?

▌ Involve the children in as much of the physical activity as possible.

▌ Composing and appreciating dance should be accessible to all children.

Finding the appropriate music is difficult?

▌ Listen to as much music as possible, e.g. travelling to work or at home.

▌ Attend to the music with an awareness of the possibilities for dance, e.g. mood music, rhythmic popular music for starting activities, classical music with dramatic themes, songs expressing imaginative ideas.

▌ Invite the children to suggest music and discuss their dance ideas at home, with a view to bringing in stimuli and resources.

▌ Use the children's own musical compositions and songs; plan to link aspects of music and dance.

▌ Develop your own musical performing skills to accompany the dance.

▌ Compile music tapes for dance and share these resources with colleagues and other schools.

The school has no money to spend on resourcing dance?

▌ Use available resources as stimuli and accompaniment.

▌ Include dance within the school development plan to ensure a financial allocation.

▌ Prioritise resources required.

SECTION FOUR

Resources for Dance

PROFESSIONAL DANCE AS A RESOURCE FOR *teaching and learning*

Children's dance education can be greatly enhanced by providing them with opportunities to view professional dance works. This may involve a live theatre visit to watch a company or individual dancer perform. Alternatively it may be possible to arrange for a dance company or artiste to be in residence within your school. This could involve the children in experience of practical workshops plus the opportunity to observe performance work. Alongside this developing provision for educational outreach work by the professional dance world, there is a gradually growing resource of professional dances on videotape available to teachers. These provide an easily accessible and relatively inexpensive

opportunity to show children a wide range of different dances. These are a valuable resource which is readily available and they have the potential to be used in a variety of ways when teaching dance.

Professional dance on video.
What is available?

The dance works selected for presentation on video are varied and eclectic. The range includes:

▮ classical ballet performed by large dance companies, e.g. *The Tales of Beatrix Potter* by the Royal Ballet

▮ excerpts from well-known ballets, featuring highly acclaimed dancers

▮ performance and discussion of specific dance styles in a cultural context, e.g. *The Path*, which explores the development of Afro-Caribbean dance

▮ contemporary dance featuring several well-known choreographers and dance companies, e.g. *Different Steps* – Rambert Dance Company; *Forest* and *Waterless Method of Swimming Instruction*, by Robert Cohan for London Contemporary Dance. Many of

these include discussions with the choreographers which act as programme notes and provide valuable contextual details.

▮ contemporary dance performed by small professional groups, e.g. *Voices* by Janet Smith

▮ dance analysis, which looks at specific features of the work, e.g. 'Rushes' by Siobhan Davies

▮ dances composed to be used intentionally as a teaching resource; these are usually accompanied by notes and work cards

▮ musicals which feature dance performed in a range of different styles, e.g. Fred Astaire films, shows such as *West Side Story* or *Grease*

How can I use it?

It is essential to be explicit about the function of the video material when planning your dance lessons. The diagram on page 65 highlights some of the areas which may be initiated or supported through access to professional dance work. The same extract may be used for different reasons within a variety of dance lessons, however, your objectives should be clear. The following are merely suggestions and there are countless other possibilities which can be explored.

Remember:
You can add to your video library by recording dance from the television, also suitable extracts from films and arts programmes which could supplement your resources.

Composing

Show the children a short extract, lasting between one and two minutes, that demonstrates how the choreographer has taken a *movement motif* and varied and developed its content, e.g. *Waterless Method of Swimming Instruction*, choreographed by Robert Cohan, explores a range of water-based activities. In this dance the literal swimming strokes are varied in many different ways, such as changing their direction and level, adding jumps and turns, performing them with dynamic variations. This could stimulate and extend their own choreographic ideas developing imaginative responses and shifting them from the literal to a more symbolic form of representation.

Using the same video select a section which uses the idea of synchronised swimming where several movements are repeated and the choreographer employs *unison* and *canon* to add visual interest to the group relationships. Many of the movements are quite simple but their effectiveness is increased by the choreographic elements. The children could work in small groups to compose their own synchronised sequence having seen the effect that moving in unison and canon can create. This would also necessitate clarity of body action and accurate timing, and if the children's work could be videotaped, these points could be discussed in relation to their own work.

Performing

The performing skills demonstrated by professional dancers may initially seem daunting due to their complexity and the high level of proficiency required to attempt them. However, they provide *exemplars* of *quality* which children may never have seen before. The physical strength, flexibility and co-ordination, combined with expressive qualities exemplified by the dancers can motivate and inspire children to raise the standard of their own performance. Male dancers can provide positive role models for boys who can associate with their obvious physical prowess.

Specific skills may be identified and developed through watching an extract in which they feature, e.g. in *The Tales of Beatrix Potter* performed by the Royal Ballet, the dance performed by Jeremy Fisher provides some inventive examples of *jumping*. It includes take off and landings on one and two feet, demonstrates a variety of body shapes in elevation and sequences of jumps with fluent transitions and accurate co-ordination. The children could be encouraged to draw some of the leg shapes they have seen Jeremy perform whilst jumping and then attempt some themselves.

Working in two's they could observe each other and comment on the line of their partner's body in the air and whether it matches the drawing. A sequence of jumps could be composed for inclusion in a dance framework related to the Tale of Mr. Jeremy Fisher (see page 67).

Using this extract a short section of the dance could be taught directly to the children. A suitable phrase is Jeremy's 'recovery' from the lake when he gently flexes his feet and legs, and shakes the water off, making sure everything is still in working order. Learning this *technical study* would require the children to pay attention to the details of the action content and sequence their movements accurately. They should also be encouraged to perform with an awareness of the expressive features as Jeremy's sadness turns to a renewal of his former vigour and joy.

Appreciating

Through guided viewing children's attention can be drawn to certain features of the dance. The development of their sensory perception, use of imagination and involvement of feelings will enhance their *interpretation* and *understanding* of the dance, e.g. in the opening section of *L'Enfant et Les Sortilèges* choreographed by Jiri Kylian, the dancer performs as an angry child using actions which typify this mood. The movements use dynamic contrasts to explore the tension within the child and the recognisable gestures, such as making a fist, drumming the fingers and tearing at his hair are everyday actions associated with anger. The children could discuss how the audience knows the mood of the dancer by identifying the gestures and expressive manner in which they are performed. This would lead to them interpreting the meaning of this extract and assist their understanding of the dance.

Certain *stylistic features* can be highlighted through watching dances from different countries or performed in different contexts, e.g. as part of a musical or in a ballroom. An extract showing the Rock 'n Roll can demonstrate the energy and vitality of this dance style, together with the rhythmic awareness and co-ordination skills essential to dance it convincingly.

You will need to place the video player and monitor in the most suitable space, the classroom or the hall, so that the children can watch easily in comfort.

Remember:

❚ Clarify your *objectives* in using the video;

❚ *Select* an appropriate extract to support the children's learning;

❚ Place the extract in a *context* so that the children have some understanding of the whole dance;

❚ If appropriate show a *complete* dance;

❚ Decide *when* to use the video in the lesson. It may be most useful to:

● show it in the classroom, before the practical activity starts;

● start the dance lesson by watching the extract;

● involve the children in selected starting activities and then show the video, but avoid sitting and talking for too long or the benefits of the starting activities will be lost;

● engage the children in their own movement exploration and show the video to stimulate and develop their ideas;

● watch the video and then allow the children to replay it and refer to it throughout the lesson as they feel necessary;

● show the professional work after their own dance is completed, to note the differences and similarities.

Diagram Showing Professional Dance as a Resource for Teaching and Learning

Theme – exploration of the theme of the dance through other sources e.g. reading, poems, discussion

Style – using the dance to compose their own work with suitable stylistic characteristics

Staging – the contribution of costumes, props and stage design to dance ideas

Stimulus – a starting point for the children's own dances

Accompaniment – listening and discussing the music/sounds, composing their own accompaniment

Improvisation – using ideas in the dance to explore new movement material

Review – critical study of the dance, this could place it within a specific cultural and historical context

Professional Dance Work

Composing – study of the choreographic content e.g. the variation of a motif; repetition of movements; the use of unison or canon

Appreciating – developing an awareness of expressive nuances and performance qualities, e.g. phrasing, focus, extension, dynamic contrast

Performing – developing and acquiring technical skills, e.g. learning a technical study taken from selected movements in the dance, concentrating on a limited range of movement material.

Remember – attention to the intrinsic expressive qualities and stylistic characteristics of the dance will promote an accurate interpretation in the performance of the study

TOPIC WEB
'JEREMY FISHER'

tales of
Beatrix Potter

The Dance is used as the topic from which other areas of the curriculum develop their schemes of work.

Arts

Dance   – Based on video
Music   – Listen to music
                 Create sounds
                 Accompany dance
Visual Art – Prints/Washes/Collage

Science/Technology

Template   – Moving frog (arms and legs)
Levers/Pulleys   – Fishing rod
Magnetism   – Fishing
Separation of Liquids – Pond Water

P.E.

Flight
Travel   – Pathways
Symmetry – Shape

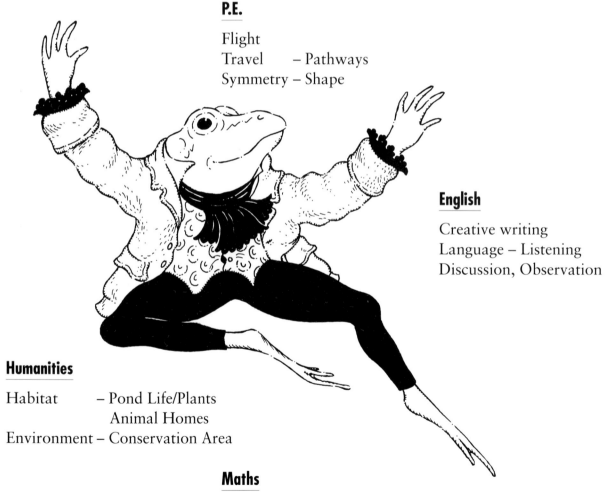

English

Creative writing
Language – Listening
Discussion, Observation

Humanities

Habitat   – Pond Life/Plants
                   Animal Homes
Environment – Conservation Area

Maths

Tessellation of Shape   – Lily Pads, Pond Life
Symmetry/Asymmetry – Leg shapes
Recording – Graphs – Height/Distance of jumps
Measuring

PLANNING A DANCE *framework*

1 Ideas Associated with the Stimulus

Literal fishing actions

Unusual body shapes in elevation

Contrast in mood

Various jumps, hops and leaps

Stimulus
JEREMY FISHER

Clear characterisation

Music/Accompaniment
From the video – 'Tales of Beatrix Potter'

Style of Dance
Dramatic/Narrative

2 Possibilities for Movement Exploration

PERFORMING SKILLS

Action phrases using jumps with clear leg gestures.

Literal actions using fishing as a stimulus.

Performing movements with the appropriate dynamics to suit the character's mood and feelings.

COMPOSITION

Linking steps together and repeating the motif.

Composing a sequence of movements.

Using contrast in dynamics to highlight specific moods and feelings.

3 A Sample Dance Framework – Composing the Movement

A Solo -
- 'Virtuoso' motif based upon a variety of jumps to show physical and technical skill.
- Travelling sequence 'across the lily pads'.
- Fishing – literal actions based upon using a fishing rod.
- Plunge into the water and recovery – to include a taught sequence based upon Jeremy's recovery on the river bank (technical study).
- Repeat of 'Virtuoso' motif.

THE TALE OF *Mr Jeremy Fisher*

from the Tales of Beatrix Potter

VIDEO APPRECIATION

This may involve the whole class, or small groups watching the video, discussing and analysing what they have seen and recording their description and interpretation through words and pictures. The following questions provide a structure for their viewing. These could be adapted depending upon the age and experience of the children.

▌ Briefly write an *outline* of the story told in this dance.

▌ How does the dance *start* and *finish*?

▌ *How* do you think Jeremy Fisher *feels* at the start of his dance? Try to think of five different words to describe his feelings.

▌ *What movements* does the dancer perform to show how he feels at the beginning of the dance?

▌ Watch carefully to see how many *different jumps* Jeremy Fisher does. *Draw* the leg shapes of three jumps – label them symmetrical or asymmetrical.

▌ At the start of the dance *how* does Jeremy dance, is it fast or slow, smooth or bouncy? Try to write some more words which could *describe how* he dances.

▌ *Describe* the *music* at the start of the dance. Try to think of five different words to describe how it sounds.

▌ Which part of the dance *stands out* in your mind? Say why.

▌ *Which movements* are most often *repeated* during the dance?

▌ Do you think the music and the movements suit each other? Give an explanation for your answer.

▌ Did you enjoy the dance? Give at least three reasons for your answer.

DANCE ARTISTES IN *residence*

What is a dance residency?

This term can be applied to professional artistes working in schools in a variety of different ways. Many dance companies have comprehensive educational programmes and dance officers who value the partnership potential of working in schools. There are also professional dance artistes working within the community who may provide specific educational expertise.

It may involve a large scale dance company, e.g. Northern Ballet Theatre or a small touring company, e.g. Adventures in Motion Pictures, or an individual dancer working in a variety of different ways in schools.

It may
- extend from half a day to a week;
- focus on one or more schools involved in individual or collaborative projects;
- involve working alongside one or more teachers;
- include children from one class or a variety of age ranges;
- incorporate a practical dance workshop focusing on technique or composition; elements of theatre design such as lighting, staging and costume; the children working towards a simple performance, the dancers dancing with the children or the company performing aspects of their repertoire.

Why have a dance residency?

A residency may be planned to realise certain aims and fulfil specific needs.

It may

▋ inspire and motivate the school community to become involved in dance;

▋ introduce children and teachers to the professional theatre world of dance;

▋ enrich and extend their knowledge and understanding of composition, performance and appreciation of dance;

▋ provide exemplars of a range of dance styles, techniques and stimuli;

▋ act as an agent of inservice training;

▋ present positive role models which encourage young people to follow a career in dance or engage in it as a lifelong pursuit;

▋ offer a focus for cross-curricular projects;

▋ develop opportunities to share ideas and present their dances to other schools;

▋ provide a means of developing your dance resources, e.g. music, video material, a cross-curricular project.

How do you plan a dance residency?

Successful residencies include the following features:

▋ clearly identified aims and outcomes;

▋ a well-planned, realistic financial budget;

▋ sensitive selection of an appropriate company or dance artiste;

▋ collaborative planning and agreed ways of working between all parties;

▋ realistic and well-defined expectations;

▋ specific and agreed criteria for review and evaluation.

Aspects to consider

It would be advisable to:

▋ consult widely before selecting the company or dance artiste to ensure they will fulfil your needs;

▋ seek the support of the advisory and support services in your LEA;

▋ involve governors, parents and the local community whenever possible;

▋ keep well-documented records of the agreements made between you and the company.

BBC DANCE *programmes*

School Radio offers a range of dance programmes for Key Stages 1 and 2 that are ideal for the non-specialist teacher. There are three series for the different age groups, all written by dance specialists, to offer a complete resource that is lively and easy-to-use and in line with National Curriculum requirements. All the programmes are tried and tested in a variety of schools before they are broadcast.

Let's Move! introduces a variety of creative movement and dance activities to children between the ages of four and six. Each broadcast is presented as a complete movement session, using a range of stimulus material: stories, such as 'The Snowman' or 'Anancy Spiderman'; infant topics, such as 'Minibeasts' or 'The Seaside'; or specific dance ideas, like 'Colour' or 'Shapes and patterns'. Music is used to stimulate and accompany the movement activities. The emphasis is on short, well structured pieces which have been especially written for dance.

Time to Move for six- to eight-year-olds, develops the skills learnt in *Let's Move!*, although it can be used independently. All programmes kick off with an energetic warm-up, which is followed by carefully structured movement content for solo, paired and group work. Themes include special adaptations of stories such as 'Toad of Toad Hall' to present as finished dance-dramas, as well as movement-inspired programmes such as 'Shake, wriggle and stroll' and 'Fiery footsteps', to help this age-group explore and experiment with different movement ideas. All the music has been specially written for the broadcasts, and reflects a broad range of styles, to include adaptations of classical music as well as up-to-the-minute synthesised dance sounds, South American salsa and much more!

Dance Workshop continues and develops the work of *Let's Move!* and *Time to Move*, but has its own exciting and distinctive style suitable for nine- to twelve-year-olds. The Autumn and Spring terms encourage the development of creative dance skills, to a range of upbeat and contemporary music: the latest in dance, hip-hop and soul, as well as bhangra, reggae, traditional ethnic, classical, folk and rock and roll! Dynamic and exhilarating – all programmes build to form a finished dance, inspired by seasonal themes such as Divali and Chinese New Year as well as popular junior topics: the rain forests, Ancient Egypt and even football! Check out a stylish Pharaoh rap, an emotional rain forest lamentation dance and a variety of street-wise dances . . . This is the perfect resource for motivating even your most reluctant top juniors!

Each Summer term's broadcasts provide a change of dance style in the form of an exciting package of traditional folk dances, from Britain and the rest of Europe.

All three series have accompanying teacher's notes, offering a detailed analysis of the programme movement and a selection of ideas to help you extend and evaluate the programme content. Contact BBC Education Information, White City, London W12 7TS. (Telephone 081 746 1111)

SECTION FIVE

Lesson Plans and Dance Frameworks

DANCE *Module 1*
KEY STAGE 1

STIMULI Poetry
Balloons

1 Module Aims

Composing – rhythmic phrases of movement, individually and with a partner.

Performing – with an awareness of the contrast between strong/light movements.

Viewing – perceive simple form and dynamics in dance.

2 Individual Dances and Specific Resources

▌ *'Pitter Patter'*

Accompaniment – the words of the poem, appropriate percussion instruments or piano

▌ *'Rain, rain go away'*

Accompaniment – the words of the poem, appropriate percussion instruments or piano

▌ *Balloon Dance*

Music with contrasting sections

Accompaniment – 'Tuba Smarties', Mike Oldfield

Resource – balloons

Stimulus

The poem:

'PITTER PATTER'

Pitter, Patter, Pitter, Patter,
Listen to the rain,
Pitter, Patter, Pitter, Patter,
On the window pane.

Music/Accompaniment

Starting activities – Ragtime music,
e.g. Scott Joplin

The dance – Words of the poem:
these may be said aloud, recorded,
used as written or certain lines
repeated.

Tambourine: this may be played by
the children or the teacher to define
the rhythm.

Objectives

Composing – rhythmic phrases of
movement.
Performing – with an awareness of
lightness in the quality
of movement
Viewing – movements which
follow a rhythmic beat.

Dance Framework

Start on own, create a phrase of
movements using the fingertips to tap
a rhythm to the words of the poem.
Repeat.

Perform a travelling phrase to the
rhythm of the words.

In two's repeat the travelling phrase,
moving away from and back towards
partner.

Establish a clear starting and
finishing position.

Starting Activities

▌ Body parts – copy teacher, circle, shake, lift and lower isolated parts of the body; include use of levels and movements away from and in towards the body.

▌ Travelling – simple steps and walks away from and towards the teacher, vary speed fast/slow – include moments of stillness when children hold their body shape.

▌ Stretching – sitting curl and extend the spine, feet, whole body.

Creating the Dance

▌ Read the poem – discuss the words, stress the lightness suggested by 'pitter patter' – say the poem together.

▌ Vary the speed of the words – establish a rhythm – use the floor, the air, parts of the body to beat against.

▌ Start on the floor in a clear position – create a simple movement motif, use the fingertips to lead the movement up and down, hold clear body shapes in silences. Repeat.

▌ Explore running and walking travelling steps, vary directions and speed. Create a simple travel motif using the word rhythm. In two's, travel away from and back towards your partner. Children may dance in unison or canon; A may lead B.

Teaching Points

▌ Name the parts as the children move them; gradually allow children to perform own movements as teacher calls out the body part.

▌ Emphasise the light quality of movement.

▌ Include pauses in the poem.

▌ The words may be said by the children and/or teacher. Encourage reaching out into the space.

▌ The children could 'accompany' their partners' travel phrase by saying the words, clapping or playing some percussion to the rhythm.

Stimulus

The poem:

Rain, Rain, Go away,
Come again another day.
Rain, Rain, Go away
Come again on washing day.

Music/Accompaniment

Starting activities – As for dance 'Pitter Patter'

The dance – The children may create a musical accompaniment of their own, stressing the contrasting dynamics and moods in the two poems.

Objectives

Composing – rhythmic phrases of movement. Individually and in two's.

Performing – with an awareness of the contrasts between strong/light movements; showing clear body shapes.

Viewing – appreciate simple dance form ABA; recognise the expressive possibilities in movement.

Dance Framework

1   Start on own, three stamps, hold a strong body shape. Repeat.

2   With partner three claps or jumps or stamps, hold a strong body shape with partner. Repeat.

Perform 1 again.

Starting Activities

▌ Children rub body parts as teacher calls them out.

▌ Travelling – light, swift runs, varying direction big steps, high knees.

▌ Jumps – bouncy jumps on the spot, hops and jumps travelling.

▌ Stretches – standing, hold a side stretch, step into a lunge.

Creating the Dance

▌ Recall 'Pitter Patter' – read new poem, discuss the contrast in feeling and words. Stress the strength in the new poem. As before establish a clear rhythm.

▌ Explore strong body shapes – use words 'go away', use different levels. Select two to show.

▌ Explore strong walks and stamps, vary directions.

▌ Create a phrase of three walks/stamps and hold a strong body shape – Repeat (A).

▌ In two's explore strong body shapes, with or without contact; may copy partner, on the floor or standing.

▌ In two's perform three claps/stamps/jumps on the spot and hold a body shape – Repeat (B).

▌ Perform whole dance – ABA.

Teaching Points

▌ Stress vigorous rubbing.

▌ Light quality.

▌ Strong quality.

▌ Angular positions, wide base for support. Half the class show, half the class watch.

▌ Emphasise control on landing, use voice or percussion to create phrases of three and hold still.

▌ Depending on the children's ability select appropriate movement tasks.

Stimulus

drift   pop

float   **Balloon**   settle

bounce   crumple

burst

Music/Accompaniment

Music with contrasting sections e.g. Mike Oldfield, 'Tuba Smarties'

Words, Percussion Instruments

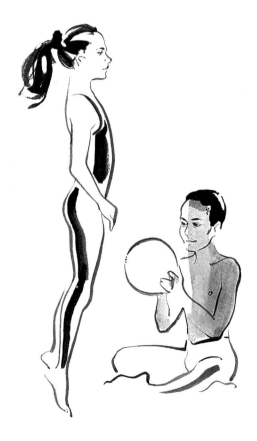

Objectives

Composing – repeat movement phrases, individually and in two's; question and answer.

Performing – with an awareness of sustained, controlled movements, sudden quick movements, and clear body shapes.

Viewing   – an appreciation of sustained, and, sudden movement qualities.

Dance Framework

▮ Select a relaxed floppy shape to represent a balloon! Long, thin, twisted, curved or rounded. Slowly inflate the balloon shape so that the body becomes larger.

▮ Create a travelling and turning phrase to suggest the release of air.

▮ Repeat both phrases.

▮ Create a phrase using bouncing gestures, steps and jumps. Stress simple directions.

▮ In two's, Dancer A performs 'bouncing' phrase around partner. Dancer B directs partner moving on the spot.

▮ The balloon bursts! Explode with a jump – crumple onto the floor to finish.

Starting Activities

▪ *Body parts* – Copy teacher bouncing feet, knees, arms, elbows, hands.

▪ *Statues* – Travel in the space, when directed hold a still position.

▪ Repeat showing *two* different shapes.

▪ Turn and spin on the spot.

▪ Travel and turn ending close to the floor.

Creating the Dance

▪ Show the children different balloons, inflated and deflated. Inflate a balloon – let it go!

▪ Individually, create a repeatable phrase showing how the body can get larger. End in a clear shape.

▪ Travel and turn onto the floor to show the balloon deflating.

▪ Create a phrase starting with bouncing in a circular pathway, add a change of direction – forwards, backwards etc.

▪ In two's, one performs, one directs. Repeat.

▪ Class to explode their balloons with a jump, turn and crumple on to the floor.

Teaching Points

▪ Use rhythmical repetitive music 4/4 count.

▪ To encourage stillness stop the music or use percussion or sound. Introduce the children to long, thin, curved, twisted or rounded shapes.

▪ Ask the children to observe a partner and describe the two shapes.

▪ Ensure that the children turn to their right and left.

▪ Fluid controlled movement phrase.

▪ Ask them to describe the shapes and why balloons increase in size! Brainstorm language ideas.

▪ Focus on sustained movement quality and control.

▪ Stress fluency of movement.

▪ Ask the children to observe their partner's phrase and describe the directions or pathway.

▪ Dancer A dances around partner B who directs with hand, arm and leg gestures.

▪ Sudden movement and clear body shape.

DANCE *Module 2*
KEYSTAGE 1 OR 2

STIMULUS   Story: 'James and the Giant Peach,' by Roald Dahl
(See notes on page 81)

1 Module Aims

Composing – action phrases which focus on travelling.

Performing – with an awareness of the speed and weight of movements, individually and in two's.

Viewing – looking at body shapes, particularly in relation to a partner.

2 Individual Dances and Specific Resources

▪ Journey into the Peach
▪ Animals in the Peach
▪ Floating to Safety

Accompaniment
● This may include percussion music created by the children, recorded and used to accompany the dance.

● Atmospheric pre-recorded music, e.g. electronic sounds, Jean Michel Jarre.

● Live music played by members of the class and/or the teacher.

STIMULUS   Story: e.g. 'James and the Giant Peach'

Having read a story the children may well be involved in a broad variety of learning activities related to the ideas, images and issues contained within it or which result from discussion about it. The dances which are composed may arise from a range of starting points, e.g.

▌ following the storyline quite literally for all or part of the dance, e.g. the journey along the tunnel;

▌ creating the mood/atmosphere suggested by the story, e.g. fear at entering the tunnel;

▌ taking on the characteristics of someone or something in the story, e.g. James himself, one of the creatures.

The dance should become a unified role, even though it may have been composed in several shorter sections. The transitions between each part of the story should be considered carefully. Opportunities may be created for the children to work individually, in two's, small groups or as a whole class. Throughout the lessons the children should be encouraged to develop their own ideas and dance phrases. They should not attempt to literally 'become' things or people in the story but be provided with movement tasks which allow them to explore the actions, dynamics and spatial features which may represent the ideas they wish to express and communicate. For example, as a spider the extension and contraction of body parts can be composed into a simple movement phrase, noting the speed and strength which would be most appropriate, i.e. the characteristics of the creature's movement can be identified and used to represent it in a dance form.

Stimulus

The story:

Journey into the Peach

Music/Accompaniment

Starting activities – Lively, rhythmic music, e.g. James Galway – *Brian Boru's March*

Objectives

Composing – a travelling sequence using a variety of body parts.

Performing – with an awareness of body shape and in relationship with a partner.

Viewing – clarity of body shapes.

Dance Framework

▌ Journey along the tunnel – changing body shape and ways of travelling.

▌ In two's travel through a tunnel made by your partner. This could develop into fours or the whole class.

▌ End by 'hitting head' on peach stone.

Starting Activities

▌ On the spot, walking in time to the music, travel about the room and return to the same spot – include skipping and galloping, add clapping.

▌ Stretching and twisting – copy teacher, use the idea of tying yourself in a knot and gradually undoing it.

Creating the Dance

▌ Introduce the idea of James's journey along the tunnel.

▌ Sit and feel the shape of the tunnel – use hands, feet, elbows, etc. Imagine the tunnel is very small and narrow – how would your body react? How would it react if it was large and wide?

▌ Explore travelling along the tunnel – show the shape and dimensions of the tunnel by the shape and manner of travel. Create a travelling sequence through three different sections of the tunnel. Show a partner.

▌ In two's explore ways of creating a 'tunnel' for your partner to travel through – create a phrase of A tunnel/B tunnel and repeat. This could build into a whole class tunnel.

▌ Decide on own ending – 'hitting head' on peach stone.

Teaching Points

▌ Stress spatial awareness about the room.

▌ Encourage awareness of body parts.

▌ Encourage descriptive language, particularly specific to movement.

▌ Words such as creep, wriggle, roll, crawl, squeeze, slide, rush etc. may be used by the teacher or written on flash cards. Stress clear body shapes and variety of speeds.

▌ Emphasise the need to link the movements smoothly to create a phrase.

Stimulus

The story:

Minibeasts in the Peach

Music/Accompaniment

Starting activities – lively rhythmic music, e.g. country dance tunes such as a polka. Contrast with slower, sustained music to accompany stretching, e.g. Enya, Vangelis

Objectives

Composing – a movement phrase using extension and contraction.
Performing – in unison with a partner and in contact with them.
Viewing – sensitivity required to work with a partner.

Dance Framework

▌ Minibeast Dance – In two's copy and perform a phrase in unison based upon stretching and contracting e.g. Spider.

▌ A's travel

▌ B's travel

▌ A/B travel together

Starting Activities

▮ Walking in straight lines, curved lines, add runs.

▮ In two's follow your partner – change leaders.

▮ Copy teacher – swinging and circling body parts and the whole body.

▮ Sitting stretching sequence – stretch spine, hamstrings, feet etc.

Creating the Dance

▮ Discuss minibeasts in the peach – how would they move, select one, e.g. spider and consider its range of movement (stretching, swinging, dangling, spinning etc.).

▮ Individually explore body shapes which are rounded and gradually extend and open out.

▮ In two's create a phrase of three stretches out and in which A/B copy each other – stress the light quality of movement.

▮ Travel on your own – use various body parts and different speeds.

▮ Explore travelling together as a spider – perhaps invent your own creature.

▮ Stay in contact with your partner.

Teaching Points

▮ Stress the need to observe your partner carefully.

▮ Create a sequence that children can copy and repeat.

▮ Depending on the minibeast discuss the quality of movement, e.g. spider is light and quick, earthworm is slower and more undulating, or get children to create their own minibeast.

▮ Encourage creativity, suggest different parts in contact with the floor or each other to increase range of ideas. Show unusual and interesting movements – select some for the class to copy.

Stimulus

The story:

Floating to Safety

Music/Accompaniment

Starting activities – lively rhythmic music, e.g. 'Pot Black' (TV Snooker Theme)

Objectives

Composing – a phrase of gestures and travelling steps, using different speeds.

Performing – with an awareness of the speed/weight of movement.

Viewing – the changing dynamics of movement and their expressive qualities.

Dance Framework

▌ Floating phrase of movement on the spot – may include rolling and sinking.

▌ Travelling phrase – perform in canon through the class.

▌ Final position – as an individual within the group.

Starting Activities

▌ Rubbing body parts – individually and in two's, carefully warm up your partner's arms, back, feet etc.

▌ In two's copy your partner's movement of body parts. Recap on stretching sequence – it may be appropriate to add some rolling actions.

▌ Walking and running steps – develop with the introduction of transferring weight onto the floor and rolling, back onto feet again.

Creating the Dance

▌ Recap on dance so far – discuss the ending of the story, use the idea of floating away to safety.

▌ Explore gently lifting arms and allowing them to 'float' down – in two's touch your partner and see if they can allow that part of them to float, e.g. knees, shoulders, fingers.

▌ Individually select three body parts which will 'float' one after the other – let it lead into light running steps.

▌ Number children one to four, perform floating phrase and travel in canon, one's start, two's next and so on – establish a finishing position.

▌ Decide on a whole class group shape to finish – rounded body shapes like the peach.

Teaching Points

▌ May start sitting in one circle, or an inner/outer circle.

▌ Emphasise need to allow partner time to copy and repeat the movements.

▌ Teach careful transference of weight onto the floor.

▌ It may be necessary to perform the dance or merely talk the story through.

▌ Work on the quality of movement.

▌ May include rolls, whilst on the spot or when travelling.

▌ Allow time to perform the *whole* dance – discuss the links between each section of the story – discuss the overall effect of the dance.

DANCE *Module 3*
KEYSTAGE 1 OR 2

STIMULUS Emotions and Feelings: Learning about myself

1 Module Aims

Composing and repeating simple movement phrases, working alone and with a partner.

Performing travelling steps and developing an awareness of individual body parts.

Viewing dance to perceive how movement may express feelings and emotions within a simple dance form.

2 Individual Dances and Specific Resources

These may be performed separately or as a series of dances. The use of children's poetry, stories, art work, sounds, music and drama ideas will enhance this stimulus.

▌ *Feeling Angry*
Accompaniment – A variety of percussion instruments, words and sounds.
Resources: Video – *L'Enfant et Les Sortilèges*, Jiri Kylian

▌ *Feeling Kind*
Accompaniment – gentle, lyrical music
e.g. Enrico Morricone – Chi Mai
      Enya – Watermark
      Vangelis
      James Galway

▌ *Feeling Happy*
Accompaniment – lively, bouncy music
e.g. Country Dance Music
      4/4 Time
      Mr Men Happy Song
      Popular Dance Music
Resources – props, bright coloured ribbons made out of material or crêpe paper

Stimulus

Emotions and Feelings:

FEELING ANGRY

Music/Accompaniment

Sounds and words: Temper, Furious, Frustration, Cross!

Percussion instruments: drums, cymbals, tambourine, wood-blocks

Objectives

Composing – repeating simple motifs working with a partner, using action and reaction.

Performing – strong travelling steps, gestures and jumps.

Viewing – observing how strong movements and shapes can be expressive of anger.

Dance Framework

▌ Three travelling stamps and freeze in a strong angular shape. Repeat the dance motif.

▌ Slow turn on spot followed by an explosive jump and strong ending position.

▌ Partner dance – action – reaction phrase using isolated gestures. Repeat.

▌ Whole group shake, tremble, building up to a class frenzy!

▌ Finish with a jump, collapsing onto the floor.

Use of Video: *L'Enfant et les Sortilèges*

▌ Watch extract showing the angry little boy.

▌ Discuss how the actions and feelings interrelate.

▌ Teach specific movements, e.g. rocking on seat, slapping hands on ground, pull a face, stamp and kick!

Starting Activities

▌ Move body parts, firmly, stress knees, elbows, fists and flexed feet.

▌ Walk around the space to the rhythm of the drum. Hold still shape when the beat stops.

▌ Develop into running. Add a turn and jump.

▌ Discussion with children; what makes us feel angry? How do we show anger? Draw up an angry word bank.

Creating the Dance

▌ Explore stamping steps varying the direction. Stress the body parts above.

▌ Create a dance motif, three stamps and hold, using the voice to accompany movements. Temper Temper Temper!

▌ Explore turning and jumping. Select one turn and jump. Accompany with
F...U...R...I...O...U...S

▌ In two's, poke fun using words (cross angry) simple gestures and clear positions. Create a repeatable phrase.

▌ Shake different body parts to include whole body, building up to a crescendo... **Frrrrrustration!**

Teaching Points

▌ Copy teacher. Start sitting, rise through kneeling to standing.

▌ Start walking – gradually introduce phrase of three steps and hold.

▌ Encourage turning to the right and left.

▌ Reinforce language work – can be done in the classroom.

▌ Firm quality and body tension.

▌ Recap and practise words in two's or as a class. Vary the tempo, pitch and dynamics.

▌ Start slowly, increase speed. Practise the phrase, refine, show half the class or a partner.

▌ Encourage a range of different gestures, kick, punch, hiss.....

▌ Whole group unison, practise dynamic use of voice.

Stimulus

Emotions and Feelings:

FEELING KIND

Music/Accompaniment

Gentle, lyrical music, e.g.
Chi Mai, Enrico Morricone

Percussion instruments: e.g. chime
bars, bells, tambourine

Objectives

Composing – complementary partner
and group shapes.
Performing – sustained light steps
and gestures.
Viewing – observing the
importance of focus,
body line and shape as
a means of expressing
the feeling of kindness.

Dance Framework

▌ Slow walks to meet partner,
explore making contact shapes with
partner. Create two repeatable,
different shapes.

▌ Walk with partner to meet
another pair. Create two shapes with
contact between four dancers.

Starting Activities

▌ Gently rubbing own body parts – shoulders, hands, legs etc.

▌ In two's lifting partner's hands, arms, legs, etc. and gently lowering them.

▌ Dancer A sitting on the floor, B moves partner's head from side to side.

▌ Walk slowly around space, listen to gentle shaking of the tambourine, hold stillness when music stops. Use toes to 'draw' initials on the floor, hands to draw initials in the air.

Creating the Dance

▌ Class discussion on why we should be kind to each other, how do you feel when people are kind to you, etc.

▌ Walking towards other children, pause, focus and reach towards them. Play the music to set the mood.

▌ Work in two's to explore contact shapes – select two.

▌ Walk towards partner slowly and perform the contact phrase.

▌ In two's explore ways of walking, leading and following a partner. Create a travelling phrase changing relationships fluidly.

▌ Work in four's to explore contact shapes – select two.

Teaching Points

▌ Encourage trust, co-operation and sensitivity.

▌ Stress the control and poise, balance and tension required, curved lines and light/sustained quality.

▌ This may take place in the classroom involving language and personal and social development objectives.

▌ Emphasise clarity of body parts in contact shape and level.

▌ Use various directions and relationships, e.g. side by side, one forwards and one backwards.

▌ Stress unity and harmony between the dancers' shapes.

Stimulus

Emotions and Feelings:

FEELING HAPPY

Music/Accompaniment

Starting activities – Country Dance Music, Mr Happy Song, Scott Joplin, ragtime music or popular dance music

The dance – Country Dance music with four beats to the bar, or popular dance music

Objectives

Composing – motifs which are capable of being repeated and developed.

Performing – skipping steps, turning skills, extension of the whole body.

Viewing – how a colourful prop can enhance the dance idea.

Dance Framework

▌ Individual ribbon dance on the spot, travel using the ribbon to make patterns in the air. Repeat motif on the spot.

▌ In two's or four's 'follow my leader' skipping and galloping around the space in different directions.

▌ Whole group circle dance.

Starting Activities

∎ Bouncy, light walks and skips, changing direction smiling at each other.

∎ High and low skips, add claps, vary direction.

∎ In two's follow my leader using any of the above.

∎ In two's copy partner using various body parts.

Creating the Dance

∎ Tell partner what makes you happy, what colours are happy?

∎ Introduce ribbon, allow improvisation exploring the use of the ribbon on the spot and travelling creating clear air patterns.

∎ Teach turning phrase and a skipping sequence using the ribbon.

∎ In two's or four's explore ways of leading and following creating straight/curved floor and air patterns.

∎ Whole class forms a circle – teacher leads a variety of patterns and formations, including the previously created individual ribbon dance.

Teaching Points

∎ Listen to tempo of the music, stress the light, jaunty nature of the movements.

∎ Be sensitive to partner's needs – do not change movement too quickly.

∎ Encourage flow and clarity of line, ribbon as an extension of the arm.

∎ Structure the length of each phrase to guide the children.

∎ Use ideas from country dances e.g. skipping in and out and around, form a chain turn your partner, (do-si-do).

ADDITIONAL FRAMEWORK IDEAS FOR *nursery, reception*
KEYSTAGE 1

1 Ideas Associated with the Stimulus

Kites – using a variety of travelling steps and swooping, circling actions.

Balls, hoops, spinning tops, taking the action ideas of bouncing, rolling and turning.

Floppy dolls, using relaxed body movements.

Clockwork toys moving in a mechanical way.

Stimulus
TOYS

Skipping rope, using an imaginary rope, performing skipping tricks, travelling with a partner.

Music/Accompaniment
Percussion instruments e.g. woodblock and cymbal, tambor and vibraslap

Style of Dance
Dramatic

2 Possibilities for Movement Exploration – 'Jack in the Box'

PERFORMING SKILLS

Use of individual body parts.

Sudden and slow movements.

Awareness of high and low.

COMPOSITION

Linking three movements to make a phrase.

Use of repetition.

Awareness of the start, middle and end of the dance.

3 A Sample Dance Framework – Composing the Movement – Solo dance, 'Jack in the Box'

▮ Start in a small shape on the floor.
▮ Perform a phrase without travelling, using individual body parts. Finish with a jump, e.g. lift the head, stretch one arm, stretch the other arm, spring up and land down on the floor. Repeat this phrase. Finish standing out of the 'box'.

▮ Travel in a small circle, skipping or galloping, feeling happy to be set free.
▮ Gradually slow down, feeling tired, and return to the 'box'.
▮ Finish in the same small shape used to start the dance.

1 Ideas Associated with the Stimulus

Masks – based on 'turnip lanterns' creating happy, sad or angry faces.

Contrast between the mood and atmosphere of night and day, e.g. daydreams and nightmares.

Magic and mystery – poetry could provide imaginative ideas and a story line.

**Stimulus
HALLOWEEN**

Characters, e.g. goblins, ghosts, spooks and witches.

Music/Accompaniment
Atmospheric music, e.g. Jean Michel Jarre

Style of Dance
Dramatic

2 Possibilities for Movement Exploration: 'Witches'

PERFORMING SKILLS

Use of individual body parts.

Strong actions, holding moments of stillness.

Twisted body shapes.

COMPOSITION

Repeating a phrase of movements.

Whole class moving in unison to conclude the dance.

3 A Sample Dance Framework – Composing the Movement

▮ Circling gestures to make the magic spell – each child transformed into a 'witch'! An explosive jump could suggest this transformation.

▮ Spiky, jerky movements using distorted body shapes, move and freeze in a shape: repeat three times, stress the strength and speed of the movements.

▮ Swift runs, travelling on a broomstick over the rooftops, create curving floor patterns.

▮ Arrive in a special magical land e.g. inhabited by strange creatures; where everyone moves in slow motion; where objects come to life, etc. Explore the movement possibilities as a class.

▮ Return journey on the broomstick, repeat the runs and finish with the 'magic spell', form the whole class into a 'magic' circle dancing together.

1 Ideas Associated with the Stimulus

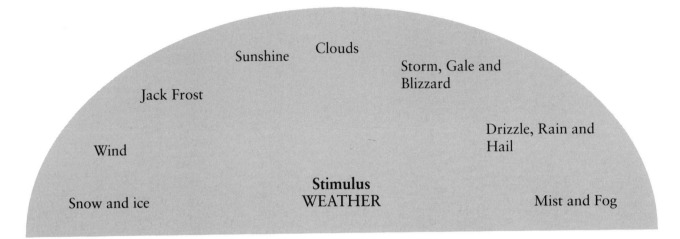

One or more of the weather ideas may be incorporated into a simple dance framework. If combining the elements look for a contrast in movement, qualities to be explored.

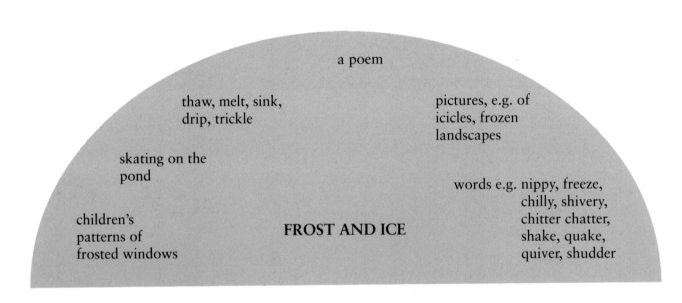

Music/Accompaniment
Graceful flowing music, words, electronic sounds

Style of Dance
Dramatic

2 Possibilities for Movement Exploration: 'Frost and Ice'

PERFORMING SKILLS

Twisted, spiky individual and small group shapes; focus on body parts. Strong tension.

Slow, careful, controlled, smooth, travelling and turning movements.

Floor patterns of little steps, hops, jumps to shake melted water away!

COMPOSITION

Combine contrasting shapes.

Simple action sequences which may be repeated.

Copy partner's/teacher's simple phrases if appropriate.

3 A Sample Dance Framework: Music/Sounds – appropriate words; 'The Blue Danube Skater's Waltz,' J. Strauss; Walking in the Air – Snowman Music.

▌ Individually create two or three twisted, spiky, icicle shapes showing contrast in levels. Emphasise body parts. Accompany each shape with a suitable frosty word.
▌ Frost – shape slowly melts by change in body tension.
▌ Tread one step carefully across the ice, pause and hold after each step. Change directions.
▌ Create a short, repeatable stepping phrase showing a change of direction.
▌ Explore ways of slow, sustained, gliding, travelling and turning movements across a frozen lake, or pond, – skating type actions. Create a short repeatable travelling phrase.
▌ Ice cracks – jump quickly to safety to finish.

1 Ideas Associated with the Stimulus

up and down movements of the pedals

props, helmets and cycle gear

sudden movement of the brakes

a bicycle for two!

Stimulus
A BICYCLE

circular, turning movements of the cogs, wheels

Music/Accompaniment
Queen: Bicycle

Style of Dance
Comical

2 Possibilities for Movement Exploration

PERFORMING SKILLS

On the spot, exploration of turning and circular body part gestures, e.g. hands, arms, legs and whole body.

Running steps with high knee lift and accompanying circular arm gestures increasing gradually in speed.

Slow motion running steps and pushing movements.

Sudden leaning forwards and backwards to stop travelling.

COMPOSITION

Repetitive phrases of gesture.

Copying and mirroring travelling movements in two's.

Encourage use of diagonals.

Working in unison in small groups.

3 A Sample Dance Framework

▮ Individually create a circular movement of the right arm gradually increasing in size. Repeat with the left arm/both arms.

▮ Whole group look right and left on the spot, before starting to ride the bicycle – could be extended with a lean.

▮ Create a travelling phrase of running steps changing direction once. Repeat. Show partner. Copy/Follow my Leader with partner.

▮ Slow motion phrase of cycle movement to represent uphill travel.

▮ Quick running steps, increasing in speed (downhill), using original, travelling phrase ideas.

▮ Stop suddenly at the crossing with a firm body shape moving forwards and backwards.

1 Ideas Associated with the Stimulus

being chased   falling

trapped   running and
                                                          getting nowhere

reaching, calling,   **Stimulus**
being ignored   **A DREAM**
                                                          lost, alone, afraid

Music/Accompaniment
A. Lloyd-Webber variations.
Poetry, dramatic stories.

Style of Dance
Dramatic/Narrative

2 Possibilities for Movement Exploration

PERFORMING SKILLS

Running, stopping in held position, looking slowly around.

Reaching upwards, (extension) to the right, left, and below (contraction).

Jumping and turning suddenly.

COMPOSITION

Create a repeatable travelling phrase showing a change(s) of direction.

Unison whole class motif.

Copy, Match or Mirror with a partner.

3 A Sample Dance Framework

Waking Up in the Dream
❚ From a still starting position on the floor, gently stir a variety of body parts moving position slightly. End by rising onto the knees and opening eyes suddenly.

Where Am I?
❚ Whole group motif. Reach with one hand and arm suddenly, as if in panic from kneeling, upwards (extend spine), downwards (contract spine), to the right and left. Repeat in unison.

Realisation – Lost?

▎ Create a short travelling phrase; running, stopping in a clear shape, slowly turning. Repeat two or three times. End in a different shape High/Low.

▎ Repeat whole group motif from standing.

Panic!

▎ Having heard a noise step backwards slowly, carefully looking from the right to the left. Use arms, hands to explore the space around.

▎ Bump into a partner, back to back. Freeze. In two's create a sudden jump with a turn to face each other. End by focusing and staring at partner.

A Happy Ending – Waking Up in Reality

▎ The person opposite is a friend. Reach out and make contact with a simple hand/arm gesture. Slowly let the strong tension disappear from the body and, smile!

DANCE Module 4
KEYSTAGE 2 OR 3

STIMULI   Clowns
Machines
Christmas Frolics

1 Module Aims

Composing phrases of movement, frequently working in two's, using the choreographic elements.

Performing with the focus on enlarged gestures, use of body parts and their relationship to the whole body shape.

Viewing dance to perceive the relevance of clear body action line and shape.

2 Individual Dances and Specific Resources

■ **Clowns**
Accompaniment – traditional fairground or circus tunes, music from the show 'Barnum', percussion
Resources – hats, baggy trousers, face masks, bow ties, props such as a hoop, bucket, ball

■ **Machines**
Accompaniment – percussive instrumental music, electronic sounds, 'house' music

■ **Christmas Frolics**
Accompaniment – seasonal, festive music
Resources – party poppers

Stimulus

Clowns:

This may form part of a series of dances on the circus.

Music/Accompaniment

Starting activities – lively, rhythmic music with a clear beat, e.g. traditional fairground or circus tunes

The dance – appropriate circus music, e.g. from the musical show 'Barnum'

Objectives

Composing – phrases of movement working with a partner, using copying and action/reaction.

Performing – a variety of running and walking steps; using enlarged gestures.

Viewing – perceiving how the dynamics of movement influence meaning, particularly in terms of characterisation.

Dance Framework

▌ Bows to the audience.

▌ Poses – 'showing off'.

▌ Funny runs around the circus ring. Repeat with partner.

▌ Duet
● A sit and clap whilst B does funny walks around them.
● Balancing act using counterbalance ideas.
● B claps, A funny walks around partner.
● Slapstick routine – action/reaction.

▌ Repeat runs to finish as the whole class travels around the circus ring.

Starting Activities

▌ Walk and clap to the music.

▌ Runs on the spot, include straight legs, bent legs, swinging legs from side to side and front to back and high knee lift etc.

▌ Travel the runs around the room, copy a partner.

▌ Stretching into a balance, tip the weight and run into another balance – use a variety of levels, rolling and turning on the floor.

Creating the Dance

▌ Create a phrase of running steps which emphasise the comic nature of a clown.

▌ Explore different partner holds, e.g. side by side, one behind the other, hands between the legs, and perform a series of running steps.

▌ Explore 'funny walks', e.g. stiff legs, jelly legs, legs tied at knees. Partner A sits and claps whilst B 'walks' around.

▌ Put dance together so far, teach bows and improvise four 'poses'.

▌ Balance/counter balance in two's, use slow motion and simple leans and balances.

▌ Develop slapstick ideas, e.g. throwing a bucket of water or custard pie in the face. Create a short action/reaction sequence.

▌ Discuss an ending, e.g. whole class runs around the circus ring.

Teaching Points

▌ Accent the beat by stressing the movement action, e.g. 1, 2, 3, 4.

▌ Encourage variety, allow children to copy and practise different types of running with flexed feet and pointed toes.

▌ Emphasise the control required to transfer the body weight and encourage the extension to come from the torso.

▌ Recall the running steps used in the starting activities.

▌ Ask the children to maintain contact with their partner whilst travelling.

▌ Half of the group watch while half perform. Look for:
  ● clarity of action
  ● rhythmical awareness

▌ Emphasise the need for control and sustained movements.

▌ Allow time for each pair to watch another duet; emphasise the need for clarity and accurate timing to ensure the sequence is effective.

1 Ideas Associated with the Stimulus

Travelling machinery

Parts of machine moving to make contact with each other

Small/large parts of the machine

Cogs and pistons

Stimulus MACHINES

Repetitive actions

Music/Accompaniment
Art of Noise
Percussion
Sound effects
Acid House or Robotic

Style of Dance
Abstract

2 Possibilities for Movement Exploration

PERFORMING SKILLS

Circling, pushing and pulling actions, using body and individual body parts.

Strong controlled movements, contrasted with quick, jerky movements.

Vary the size and level of movements, emphasise clear body shapes.

COMPOSITION

Develop rhythmic patterns of movement, capable of repetition.

Use canon to pass movements through a group or to a partner.

Create a phrase that travels using a variety of actions.

3 A Sample Dance Framework

▌ Individually create a simple phrase using two or three different body parts.

▌ Repeat, increasing the size of movements.

▌ Travel to a partner, create a phrase of action/reaction, use contrasting and complementary body shapes.

▌ Travel with partner to form a small or large group machine, pass movement through the group in canon.

▌ Machine goes out of control, increase speed, collapse!

1 Ideas Associated with the Stimulus

Snow – building a snowman, snowball fights

Skiing, skating

Nativity story

Crackers, streamers, funny hats, party poppers

Traditions across the world

Party games, Christmas frolics

Stimulus CHRISTMAS

Ballet – The Nutcracker

Music/Accompaniment
Appropriate Christmas music, e.g. Jingle Bells; So this is Christmas – John Lennon; Merry Christmas – Slade; The Snowman Reggae, bhangra or flamenco music

Style of Dance
Comic

2 Possibilities for Movement Exploration: 'Christmas Frolics'

PERFORMING SKILLS

Travelling steps, holding clear body shapes.

Enlarged gestures, emphasising body parts.

Balance and counterbalance, jumping and falling.

COMPOSITION

In two's copy and mirror body shapes.

Use canon and contrasting shapes within a small group.

3 A Sample Dance Framework

Musical Statues
▮ Individually create a phrase – travel and hold a shape, repeat two times showing contrasting body shapes.
▮ Meet a partner, A teaches B their action phrase and B teaches A; perform both phrases in unison, copying and mirroring the still body shapes.

Pass the Parcel
▮ In groups of four using exaggerated gestures and specific body parts to represent the game 'Pass the Parcel'. Contrast the shape and level from the person next to you.
▮ Repeat in the reverse direction.

Pulling the Cracker
▮ In contact with a partner create a phrase based on counterbalance, showing a contrast in level.
▮ End the dance with a party popper to signify the 'snap' of the cracker, children jump and fall.

DANCE *Module 5*

STIMULUS Traditional Folk Dance

1 Module Aims

▌ *Composing* dances which use traditional and conventional folk dance figures.

▌ *Performing* simple step patterns with an awareness of poise and rhythm.

▌ *Viewing* to perceive the conventional folk dance sets, figures and steps.

2 Individual Dances

▌ Farandole, French Chain Dance
▌ Cumberland Square Eight, Pat a Cake Polka
▌ Children's own Folk Dance

Music – Appropriate Traditional Music

Resources – English Folk Dance and Song Society books, tapes and records, ribbons, scarves, sticks, brooms

Longways Duple proper
for as many people as want to dance

⌐ 1st time through   2nd time through ⌐→

top (music)

1st couple	○ □	2nd couple	○ □	
2nd couple	○ □	resting change to 1st		
1st	○ □	1st	○ □	
2nd	○ □	2nd	○ □	
		1st	○ □	
1st	○ □	2nd	○ □	
2nd	○ □			
		1st	○ □	
		2nd	○ □	
		1st couple	○ □	
		resting change to 2nd		

in longways sets like this you keep your original numbers until you have a rest at the end

bottom

Sets/Formation

Longways set for 4 couples
(3 & 5 similar)

○ Boy □ Girl

	top (music)		
1st couple	○ □		up ↑
2nd	○ □		
3rd	○ □		
4th	○ □		down ↓

bottom

Double Circle

Square Set
all face centre music

1 + 3 are HEAD couples
2 + 4 are SIDE couples

Figures

Single arch   Double arch

Basket

Single cast   Double cast

top   top

Star (right hand)   Promenade

Grand Chain: Partners face each other and give right hands. Move forward, past partner, give left hand to next person, move past, give right hand to next, and so on, following the call.

Do-si-do: Face partner (or other dancer, as directed). Walk forward to pass right shoulders, step to right and come backwards to place passing left shoulders, all without turning around.

Forward and back: Dance forward, usually four steps and back to place.

Gallop: Side-stepping, usually with a ballroom hold, or a two-hand hold.

Swing: Turn partner round, using ballroom or cross hand hold. Each partner uses his/her right foot as a pivot (outside edges almost touching) and pushes the swing round with the left foot.

ballroom hold   *cross hand hold*

Turn: Left-hand — partners hold left hands, and dance around each other.
Right-hand — as for left-hand, but holding right hands.
Two-hand — partners facing, holding partner's right hand in own left hand and vice versa, dance around clockwise.

Arming: As turning, only linking elbows or forearms as appropriate.

1　Ideas Associated with the Stimulus

Social event

Couples, groups
of dancers

Country of origin

Community
spirit

Traditional
costume and
props

Ritual and
celebration

Focus on
participation

Stimulus
FOLK DANCE

Open air, non
theatre setting

FARANDOLE
FRENCH CHAIN DANCE

Music/Accompaniment
2/4 tune

Style of Dance
Traditional folk dance

2　Possibilities for Movement Exploration

PERFORMING SKILLS

Light, rhythmic walking and skipping steps.

Curving and straight floor patterns.

COMPOSITION

Unison step patterns.

Various group formations, dancers to hold
hands in a chain.

3　A Sample Dance Framework

▮ CHAIN DANCE
  - Walk through the various figures,
    e.g. snake or serpentine

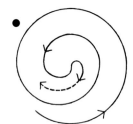
– Snail or spiral, dancers hold
hands and face inwards making a
spiral floor pattern. The leader
turns towards right shoulder to
lead the line out through the spiral.

Dancers 1 and 2 form a double arch facing each other.

Dancers 3 and 4 remain holding hands, pass in single file under the arch and then make their own double arch.

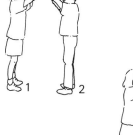

This continues until the whole class has formed arches.

Dancer 1 leads dancer 2 by the hand through the arches followed by each consecutive couple to reform a chain.

● All the dancers except the leader raise their arms to make a single arch.

Dancer 1 weaves in and out of the arches leading the chain. Dancers remain holding hands throughout.

▌ CUMBERLAND SQUARE EIGHT

Music:	'My love she's but a lassie yet', or any 32 bar reel or jig.
Form:	Square set of four couples.
A.1 and 2.	Tops: gallop across and back. Sides: the same.
B.1 and 2.	Tops: right hands across and left hands back. Sides: the same.
A.1. and 2.	Tops: form a basket. Sides: the same.
B.1. and 2.	All join hands and circle left. Promenade partner to place.

▌ PAT A CAKE POLKA

Music:	'Nick Nack Paddy Whack', 'Little Brown Jug', 'Buffalo Girls'.
Form:	Two concentric circles, men inside facing partners.
A.	Ballroom hold: To man's left: heel, toe, heel, toe, four chassés. Repeat to right.
B.	Three claps each to partner's right, to partner's left, to partner's both hands, to own knees. Each man gives his girl a right arm swing and passes her on to a new partner as he moves one place to his left.

This dance exists in many variations.

The form and progression may be used for any sequence to suit the occasion, to promote social interaction and to help beginners to get the feel of typical dance movements including partner work.

1 Ideas Associated with the Stimulus

Figures in two's
e.g. do-si-do,
promenade, swing

Group
formations, e.g.
square set, long
set, circle, double
circle, chain

Clapping in time
to the music

Simple steps
skipping,
walking,
galloping, polka

**Stimulus
CHILDREN'S
FOLK DANCE**

Figures, e.g.
single cast,
double cast, star,
basket

Music/Accompaniment
Polka, jig or reel tune

Style of Dance
Traditional folk dance using
conventional steps and figures

2 Sample Dance Frameworks
Select some of the following ideas

In two's –   Follow my leader dance
Advance and retreat
Skip in a circle
Meet and change places
Meet and swing your partner
Meet and do-si-do

In fours –   Chain dance
sixes and eights Circle dance
Set dance
Use the figures suggested above

Throughout the dance stress the need for simple steps and
floor patterns which are repeated. Use the phrasing in the
music to help structure the form of the dance. The dancers
frequently travel to the right and then to the left, forward and
back, circling clockwise and anticlockwise. The children
should be encouraged to learn both male and female parts if
relevant to the cultural context.

DANCE *Module 6*
KEYSTAGE 2 OR 3

STIMULUS   Sporting Themes

1 Module Aims

Composing simple movement motifs derived from literal movements and developed to become more symbolic.

Performing dance movements displaying a greater awareness of the range of qualitative aspects.

Viewing to perceive the dance metaphors and how they convey meaning.

2 Individual Dances and Specific Resources

▮ Swimming Pool Dance

Accompaniment – Saints Saëns – Carnival of the Animals, The Aquarium

Resources – London Contemporary Dance Theatre – *Waterless Method of Swimming Instruction* by Robert Cohan

▮ Football Dance

Accompaniment – Match of the Day, TV Theme Tune

Resources – Scarves

▮ Martial Arts

Accompaniment – Mike Oldfield, Killing Fields

Resources – Bamboo cane

Stimulus

The class topic of 'Carnival of the Animals'

Using 'The Aquarium' piece of music to create a swimming pool dance.

Music

For the dance – Saint Saëns: Carnival of the Animals, The Aquarium

For the starting activities – Lively, rhythmic music e.g. 'Dancing in the Street', by the Rolling Stones, would provide an interesting contrast to the gentle, flowing music chosen for the dance. Their different expressive qualities could be highlighted and discussed.

If possible show the children extracts from the dance video *Waterless Method of Swimming Instruction*, performed by London Contemporary Dance Theatre and choreographed by Robert Cohan.

Objectives

Composing – simple movement motifs whose actions derive from swimming strokes, creating variations of the literal movements; phrases which may be performed in unison and canon.

Performing – with an awareness of the dynamics of sudden/sustained direct/flexible, and strong/light movements.

Viewing – perceiving how the representational/ literal swimming actions have been varied and developed.

Dance Framework

The children will work individually, in two's and as part of a group of four or five.

'A Swimming Pool Dance'
▎ Activity around the poolside. Hold a starting position.

▎ In two's enter the pool.
(Use canon to allow time for each pair to enter.)

▎ Swimming motif alone and in unison with a partner.

▎ Synchronised swimming sequence in fours or fives.

▎ Floating to the poolside, finishing position in two's.

Starting Activities

❚ Listen to the music, 'The Aquarium' and describe its quality, mood, tempo and phrasing.

❚ Select vigorous activities including travelling and jumping to provide a contrast to the dynamics of the dance.

❚ Teach the children how to fall and roll onto the floor.

Creating a Dance

❚ Sitting in a space imagine you are floating in warm water. Gradually explore 'floating' with different parts of the body.

❚ Use breast stroke as an example of a swimming action. Ask the children how the arm and leg actions could be varied and developed.

❚ Ask the children to create a movement motif which travels them about the space. Select, practise and refine the motif. Show a partner – teach sequence to partner.

❚ In two's allow children to decide how they will enter the water, e.g. dive, slide, jump.

❚ Establish a clear starting position in two's around the outside edges of the dance space; perform entry into the 'pool', dance, swimming motif individually and in unison.

❚ Join with another pair and in fours create a synchronised swimming sequence.

❚ Conclude the dance by floating to the poolside and holding a finishing position in two's.

Teaching Points

❚ How can you convey the idea of moving through water? Discuss the idea of resistance.

Motif development.
● Change the direction of the arm gesture, up, down, sideways, diagonally;
● Use one side of the body and then the other so that it becomes asymmetrical;
● Alter the level from high to low use the floor, add a rolling action;
● Vary the speed of movement;
● Vary the directness of the movement flexible – direct;
● Add another action such as a jump or a turn;
● Explore ways of travelling.

Ideas may include –
● Using a circle formation
● Performing in unison and canon
● Using contrasts of speed, levels and directions in the group.
● Notate using simple diagrams.

1 Ideas Associated with the Stimulus

Referee controlling the game

Action replay

Crowds swaying and cheering with banners and scarves

Running on to the pitch

Dribble and pass

Scoring a goal

Winners and losers

Goalkeeper's moves

**Stimulus
FOOTBALL**

Throw in from the side line

Music/Accompaniment
TV tune, Match of the Day
'Offside' Mike Vickers
Football songs and chants

Style of Dance
Comic

2 Possibilities for Movement Exploration

PERFORMING SKILLS

Different running steps, actions to bend, stretch and twist the body.

Leap, fall and roll.

Slow motion and action replay.

COMPOSITION

Small groups travel in unison.

Action and reaction in two's.

3 A Sample Dance Framework

▌ In teams of four create a travelling phrase of running steps, vary the floor pattern.

▌ Individually create a repeatable 'warm up' phrase based upon bending, stretching and twisting.

▌ In two's action/reaction sequence selected from two of the following: tackle, corner, penalty kick, throwing, scoring a goal.

▌ Repeat the phrase using slow motion.

▌ Whole class conclude with a swaying and stretching motif that is rhythmic and repetitive. Scarves may be used as a prop.

Additional Resources
Video material and photographs could enhance the movement exploration.

1 Ideas Associated with the Stimulus

Eastern cultural influence, ritual, ceremony

Athletic, skilful movements

Unarmed, armed combat

Concentration, control mind and body in harmony

Stimulus
MARTIAL ARTS

Patterns of movement

Music/Accompaniment
Killing Fields:
Mike Oldfield

Style of Dance
Dramatic
ritualistic

2 Possibilities for Movement Exploration

PERFORMING SKILLS

Sustained direct movements.

Jumps, leaps and turns.

Stylised gestures.

COMPOSITION

Repeated phrases, copy and mirror a partner.

Work in two's, use of a prop, action/reaction.

Formal introduction and ending.

3 A Sample Dance Framework

A Duet

▌ Introduction – Ceremonial greeting using ritualistic gestures.

▌ Create a movement motif based upon the directions, (side/side, forward/back) mirror in two's. (Repeat two times.)

▌ Use simple steps and held gestures.

▌ Develop the motif – add a jump and/or a turn.
            – repeat the motifs using a cane.

▌ Combat sequence in two's based upon action/reaction (move around, over and under each other). Explore ways of dancing with the cane.

▌ Conclusion – Ceremonial ending which may involve the repetition of whole or part of the greeting.

DANCE *Module 7*
KEYSTAGE 2 OR 3

STIMULUS The Silent Movies

1 Module Aim

To develop an appreciation of the techniques used in characterisation in the Silent Movies, i.e. the stereotypical movements associated with The Stuntman, Hero, Heroine, Villain.

2 Individual Dances and Specific Resources

- *Dance 1* 'The Stuntpersons'
- *Dance 2* 'Movie Melodrama'

Accompaniment – 'Stuntmen' and 'Movie Melodrama' – Keystone Cops

Alternative Suggestions
> Scott Joplin, Fats Waller
> Alfred Hitchcock Film Music
> Charlie Chaplin Film Music
> Laurel and Hardy Film Music

Resources –
> video material of Silent Movie Films
> resources from 'Dash' – Wayne Sleep's Company piece
> photographs of silent movies, pictures etc. from film magazines and media centres
> pictures and photographs from magazines showing strong model poses and shapes

Stimulus

Silent Movies: The Stuntpersons!

Music/Accompaniment

'Stuntmen': Keystone Cops.

Objectives

Composing – to explore a variety of choreographic devices in the creation of a simple duo-action-reaction, canon and complementing.

Performing – to create and perform exaggerated motifs based on travel, pause and gesture portraying the dramatic quality of the character.

Viewing – to appreciate the changes of mood, qualities and atmosphere expressed in the music of this era – and the potential for dramatic interpretation.

Dance Framework

▌ Introduction: (Dancers to start off stage in two groups.) Group A enters with walks and poses. Group B repeats these moves.

▌ Partner Work-Duet of Balancing Tricks and Poses.
● Show off muscles to each other using different shapes.
● Display strength/prowess, balancing and supporting each other.
● Run, fall, jump over each other.

▌ *Finale*
Whole group, step-kick sequence and poses to finish.

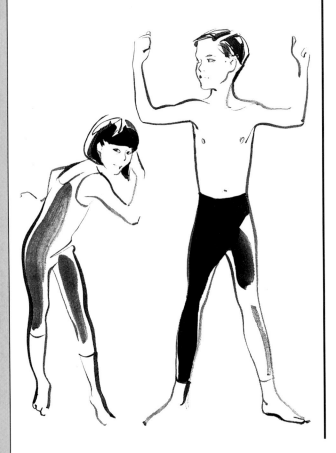

Starting Activities and Introduction to the Stimulus

▌ Use a variety of travelling steps, e.g. struts and jumps. Explore falls, rolls and balancing actions.

Creating the Dance

▌ Stuntperson enters, with travelling steps, poses to the audience, walks in a circular pathway and holds finishing shape.

▌ Individually create a motif of three strong shapes.

▌ Explore counter balance and support with a partner, e.g. stand side by side, hold hands/wrists, pull away to achieve balance with straight arms.

▌ Create a duet of poses and balancing actions. Conclude falling in a heap on the floor.

▌ Explore working with a partner running jumping over each other, showing clever falls, tricks and rolls.

▌ Select from the ideas two tricks each. Create a motif.

▌ Groups of four to six to create a 'Finale' curtain call – steps, kicks and poses.

▌ Whole group to create a short single phrase to finish in a group complementary group shape.

Teaching Points

▌ Encourage exaggerated movements of the arms, facial gestures and leg actions.

▌ Emphasise facial gestures.

▌ Use different levels and fluent transitions.

▌ Tension, control, clarity of line and shape. Firm supportive base!

▌ Fluent linking movements.

▌ Use of complementary shapes.

▌ Focus on action and reaction.

▌ Walking in lines; arms on shoulders; facing the audience low kicks; high kicks; step kicks; turns; waving hands etc.

Stimulus

Silent Movies – Movie Melodrama

Music/Accompaniment

Keystone Cops

Props
Basket, bottle, hanky, cane, seat, rope, cloak and hat.

Objectives

Composing – to create movement motifs based on travel, pause and gesture, and compose them into a dramatic scenario.

Performing – to explore exaggerated movements used to portray the dramatic quality of the characters.

Viewing – to appreciate the characteristic qualities in the music of this era – and the potential for dramatic interpretation.

Dance Framework

▌ Heroine on stage in a precious pose!

▌ Villain enters – large menacing walks, use cloak to exaggerate gestures.

▌ Heroine reacts – travels and pleads for mercy using a series of poses. Villain watches and makes gestures throughout.

▌ Hero enters using a jaunty repetitive step pattern interspersed with brave fearless poses.

▌ Heroine pleads to the hero for help.

▌ Dramatic fight scene, villain captures heroine – hero rescues her!

▌ Villain is defeated – hero and heroine dance off together.

Starting Activities

I Listen to the music.

I Discuss the qualities, atmosphere and the characters.

I Watch video if possible.

Creating the Dance

A Trio!
Ensure the children have an opportunity to dance the three characters.

I Villain enters, large walks and exaggerated gestures, three times.

I Heroine travels to four areas in the room and ends each travel with a pleading pose, four times.

I Hero arrives on the scene using a jaunty, skip like step pattern interspersed with strong 'brave' poses.

I Heroine repeats travel, pleading to the hero for help, three times.

I Fight develops between the hero and the villain. The heroine is pulled from one to the other and eventually tied to the railway track by the villain who has knocked the hero out! Teach a *set* technical study from a video if possible or ask the children to create a class motif for the fight scene.

I Hero recovers, resumes the fight, wins and rescues the heroine.

I Hero and heroine dance off together leaving the villain mortified.

Teaching Points

I Ask the pupils to create a dramatic storyline with the three characters.

I Show pictures of 1920s movie stars demonstrating stereotypical characters. Discuss the use of props and costumes.

I Strong dramatic movements.

I Light, quick, run – vary the position of the pose – floor, kneeling and standing.

I Light, repetitive, rhythmical motif contrasted with stronger held positions.

I Use of complementary shapes in the tug of war.

Action/reaction in fight between villain and hero.

Use props.

ADDITIONAL FRAMEWORK *ideas*

KEYSTAGE 2 AND 3

The Big Bang

Geological periods and a timeline

Relationships between plants, herbivores and carnivores

Links with present day crocodile

Dinosaurs

**Stimulus
EVOLUTION**

Fossils

Extinction

Accompaniment
Vangelis, 'Soil Festivities'

Reading
'Dinosaurs and all that Rubbish'

Fossils and Dinosaurs Dance

Introduction 'Big Bang', whole group explode with a jump.

Fossils – Trilobites and Ammonites

▌ Discuss shape and movement of different fossil creatures, e.g. the trilobites, sudden scuttling movements. Change the pathways and levels whilst travelling about the space.

▌ Form a whole group ammonite shape, creating a spiral pattern on the floor.

▌ Each dancer spirals up and down in canon, retaining the group 'ammonite' shape.

Dinosaurs – plant eaters, hunters, plodders, athletes, flyers etc.

▌ Roll out from the group into a rounded body shape, representing the dinosaur egg.

▌ Use different body parts to push and stretch, trying to break out of the shell, compose a phrase of three movements.

▌ Burst out of the shell and freeze in a clear body shape, e.g. spiky or rounded. (Look at pictures of dinosaurs.)

▌ Develop a travelling step for each dinosaur, vary the strength and speed of the movements. Discuss the differences between the types of dinosaur; some travelled in the air, others in the water or on land.

▌ In two's have a battle of the dinosaurs; use the idea of meeting and parting with various body parts in contact. Compose a phrase of movements that can be repeated.

▌ Extinction – travel in two's, as a larger dinosaur and form a whole class fossilised dinosaur skeleton.

1 Ideas Associated with the Stimulus

Leaping and diving actions

On board the whaling boat – machinery, firing the harpoon

Rowing a small boat, sighting the whale

Moving as if in a 'school' of whales

Chasing the whales

Whales gliding through the water

Stimulus
THE WHALE HUNT

Dramatic ending, death or escape of the whale

Music
The Whale Hunt from 'The Moving
Environment' by Philip Taylor
Atmospheric music, e.g. Jean Michel Jarre,
Gabrielle Roth

Style of Dance
Dramatic

2 Possibilities for Movement Exploration

PERFORMING SKILLS

Gliding runs using curving floor patterns.

Jumps and leaps, using arched body shapes.

Work actions on the boat – using machine-type movements, rowing, hauling and pushing ideas.

COMPOSITION

Create a clear, curving floor pattern.

Action sequence which is repeated.

Action and reaction.

Group shapes.

3 A Sample Dance Framework

❙ Individually create a curving floor pattern, travel using swift, gliding runs.

Use question and answer between the two groups

half class —
● In groups of four use work actions to represent movement on board the boat – use action and reaction, stillness holding group shapes.

❙ Compose a motif based on whales leaping and jumping – repeat it.

half class —
● In groups of four travel as a 'school' of whales in unison, using a phrase of run, leap and roll.

❙ Harpoon is fired: Conclusion – does the whale survive?

1 Ideas Associated with the Stimulus

Group identity
Tribal allegiance

Fighting skills
essential for a
warrior

Dances to
celebrate events,
e.g. war, victory,
birth, marriage

Athletic,
powerful
movement

Stimulus
TRIBAL WARRIORS

Rhythmic,
drumming music

Music/Accompaniment
The Warrior – Ipi Tombi;
Music by Hugh Masakela;
Percussion accompaniment
performed by the dancers

Style of Dance
Dramatic

2 Possibilities for Movement Exploration

PERFORMING SKILLS

Action phrases using travel, jump and
stillness.

Strong powerful and direct quality of
movement.

Clarity of body shape.

COMPOSITION

Repeated phrases of movement.

Use of action/reaction.

Group shapes, suggesting unity and power.

3 A Sample Dance Framework – Composing the Movement

▮ Individually perform a rhythmic
sound pattern: include stamps, claps,
drumming on the floor.
▮ Use the action phrase run, jump, and
freeze, holding a strong, fierce body
shape; repeat three times to meet a
partner; a shield, spear or stick could be
an 'imagined' prop.
▮ Compose a non-contact fight
sequence, using action/reaction and
contrasting body shapes; use ideas of
above and below each other, surrounding
and repelling.

▮ In two's travel in unison using a
simple, rhythmic step pattern which
repeats.
▮ In groups of four to six perform a
circle dance suggesting victory after
battle; compose step patterns which
travel around, in and out of the circle;
individual dancers perform actions
displaying physical prowess across the
circle, e.g. leaps and turns.
▮ Perform a step pattern in unison and
finish in a strong, triumphant group
shape.

1 Ideas Associated with the Stimulus

Egyptian tombs – tomb paintings

Characters, e.g. Pharaoh, Slave, Warrior, Mourner

Sandstorms

Stylised body shapes

Travel back in time through a time tunnel

Stimulus
ANCIENT EGYPT

Sphinxs, pyramids

Music/Accompaniment
'Beginnings' – Philip Taylor
'Totem' – Gabrielle Roth
'Powaqqatsi' – Philip Glass

Style of Dance
Narrative

2 Possibilities for Movement Exploration

PERFORMING SKILLS

Travelling through the time tunnel – action phrase, e.g. contract, stretch and roll, sustained movement quality.

Journey across the desert/sandstorms – action phrase, e.g. fall, twist and reach.

Stylised gestures and body shapes.

COMPOSITION

Repeated phrase of movement.

Perform in unison with a partner.

Mirror a partner's motif.

3 A Sample Dance Framework – Composing the Movement

Use pictures of Egyptian tomb paintings to illustrate typical body positions.
▮ Half the class create the 'time tunnel' by holding a series of curved/angular body shapes.
▮ The other half of the class travel over, under, around and through these shapes using their action phrase – on a given signal, change roles.
▮ In two's travel in unison through the sandstorm, using ideas of falling, twisting and reaching, use body contact.

▮ Arrive at the tomb – create a 'picture' in fours.
▮ Paintings come to life – using the illustrations of tomb paintings select three shapes to copy. Create a motif and perform in two's mirroring each other.
▮ Ending – Create a whole or half class pyramid/sphinx, stressing the symmetry of the group shape.

Dance Ideas related to a theme/topic developing cross-curricular links

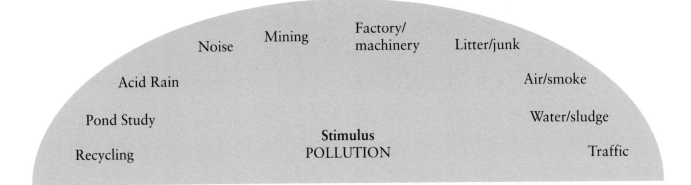

Noise Mining Factory/machinery Litter/junk

Acid Rain Air/smoke

Pond Study Water/sludge

Recycling **Stimulus** Traffic
POLLUTION

DANCE IDEAS

1 Factory Life –
Man versus
Machinery

2 Water Pollution –
using material
and streamers as
props

3 Junk Dance,
using boxes,
large cardboard
packaging etc. as
props and
composing a
'rap' to
accompany the
dance

1 Factory Life

Accompaniment – Steve Fox 'Pastiche City' or Technotronic
'This beat is technotronic'.

Man v Machinery

❚ In groups of four, each individual isolates one small
movement gesture and repeats it.
❚ In two's add your partner's movement gesture to your
own – creating a phrase of two movements.
❚ Add a larger movement to the phrase – actions that
involve up down, side-side, forward and back creating a
motif. This may be varied by changing the speed or
rhythm and developed by adding a turn, jump or travel.
Perform in unison with a partner, either copying or
mirroring, or in two's with one dancer moving their
partner and 'controlling' them.

▌ In two's A   travels to create a large group machine, possibly half the class, where the individuals move successively, initiating the next dancer's movement suggesting pistons, cogs and chains.

        B   travels to form a large group of 'operators' who create a sequence based upon pulling levers, turning wheels, pushing knobs and buttons. Perform in unison in a strong group shape.

▌ Large machine – movements gain momentum; as speed increases control is lost; each dancer uses the actions leap, turn, travel in any order to compose a phrase which 'breaks' the machine apart. Hold a 'distorted' body shape to finish.

▌ Operators – movements slow down; gradually the group disperses using a simple, repetitive step pattern to travel through the still machinery parts, conveying boredom and tedium in their movement.

2 Water Pollution

Accompaniment – Electronic music, sound effects

▌ Discuss the natural movement of water and create a word bank, including dashing, swirling, tumbling, churning, foaming, trickling, splashing to evoke images of water in motion.

▌ Explore the words using movement actions, e.g. leaping, falling, spinning, spiralling, rolling.

▌ Teach a movement motif based upon rising and falling actions.

▌ Work in two's to vary and develop the set motif.

▌ Compose the start of the dance; use the original motif and the variations; start with two couples dancing and gradually involve the whole class.

▌ Introduce lengths of material which the dancers use to create circular patterns, rising and falling movements. Allow for exploration of the movement possibilities and vary the group sizes from two to six dancers to provide different visual effects.

▌ Introduce dark coloured streamers for the dancers to move with to symbolise the pollutants, create contrasting phrases using sudden, angular, strong movements.

▌ Compose the middle of the dance, in groups of varying sizes, half the class perform movements using the lengths of material. The 'pollutants' interact with the rest of the dancers using question and answer. The flowing movements and the material overwhelm and entrap the pollutants.

▌ The dance concludes by repeating Section A; the material and streamers are discarded and the original motifs restated.

3 Junk Dance

Accompaniment – A 'rap' using the children's own ideas about the polluting effects of junk and rubbish.

▌ Provide props using large cardboard boxes, tubes, drums etc.

▌ In small groups of three and four explore ways of grouping the 'junk' to create visually interesting shapes.

▌ Use the spatial ideas of over, under, through and around to compose a movement phrase. The dynamics of the movement should reflect the tone of the accompanying rap, whether it is strong and aggressive, sad and reflective or another appropriate mood expressing the dancers' feelings about the pollution of the environment.

▌ Dance with the 'junk', creating action phrases appropriate to the prop; explore ideas passing and throwing the objects between the dancers. Use dropping, jumping and pauses to highlight the actions. Have some groups dancing while others 'rap'.

▌ Decide how the dance should finish – all 'rap' to make a strong statement on pollution; clear the space of 'junk' and create a dance in celebration using popular disco type music; sink back into the 'junk' and finish as the dance started.

Light and energy

Water in the home

Furnishings

Animal homes

House in history

Bricks and walls

Homes in other lands

Shapes and structures

Own home

Stimulus
HOMES

Ideal home

DANCE IDEAS

1 Building Site

2 Architecture – the skyline

1 Building Site

Accompaniment – Art of Noise

▮ Explore work actions, e.g. digging, sawing, hammering, lifting and carrying, which typify a building site at work. Enlarge and exaggerate the movements.

▮ Explore the movement of machines, e.g. cement mixer, pneumatic drill, chain saw.

▮ Vary the spatial and dynamic features, e.g. use the rotation of the cement mixer, take the movement down onto the floor, roll, twist and spiral, sustain the phrase so that it is in slow motion.

▮ Establish a simple rhythmic work action in two's using unison and canon.

▮ Use the idea of still poses to freeze the action, e.g. leaning on shovels.

▮ In threes and fours take one simple process, e.g. bricklaying, mixing cement, measuring and sawing, and perform with enlarged gestures using successive movements in the group.

▮ Develop the idea of a foreman inspecting the work; use action/reaction; conclude with strike action and down tools! Compose a 'still photograph' to symbolise this.

2   Architecture – the skyline

Accompaniment – Vangelis 'Missing'

▌ Look at pictures illustrating a variety of different skylines, e.g. New York, Delhi, London, African villages. Discuss the lines, shapes and contours of the buildings, how they interrelate and present a visual picture using curved and straight lines, e.g. mosque, church, Eiffel Tower.

▌ Explore different body shapes to represent the skyline contours; work in two's and three's using body contact. Use symmetry and asymmetry to encourage a variety of outlines and to suggest balance and off-balance.

▌ In fours create three different skylines, moving from one to another with interesting transitions. The ideas of silhouettes could be suggested.

▌ In two's compose a phrase of three different body shapes using contrasting and complementary shapes to symbolise the three-dimensional buildings.

▌ Use a length of string (approx. 1.5m) which is held taut between the two dancers as they repeat their phrase, to suggest the architectural lines drawn on house plans.

▌ Compose a whole class or several large group shapes involving the string to add visual interest.

▌ Conclude by repeating one of the initial skyline shapes which every group copies.

glossary

Accent – the placement of stress on one beat or movement.

Aesthetic – concerned with appreciation through using the senses with imaginative attention.

Alignment – the position of parts of the body in relation to the whole body.

Canon – a musical term used in dance composition when two or more parts recur, repeat or interrelate in time, i.e. one part is followed by another in time.

Chassé – a sideways step, moving out with one foot and closing the other one to it.

Choreography – the method of selecting and structuring movement into a dance form.

Composition – arrangement of parts to make a whole; a term applied across the art forms.

Contraction – rounding the body and pulling parts in towards the centre.

Dynamics – the energy of movement.

Ethnic Dance – the dance which originates from people of a common cultural, racial and/or religious heritage.

Extension – stretching out from the centre of the body.

Folk Dance – the dance associated with a particular country, often part of a traditional celebration and linked with nationalistic feelings.

Form – the overall design for patterning the movement, its shape and structure.

A Gallop – a leap in uneven rhythm.

Highlight – a part of the dance which is designed to 'stand out' from the rest by virtue of its originality, impact, etc., providing a noticeable feature within the whole.

Improvisation – a child's initial movement response to an idea or stimulus. This will be determined by their level of skill and range of movement vocabulary interacting with their imagination. This can be developed by structuring tasks within a framework.

Legato – smooth, flowing style, the opposite of staccato.

March – regular walking steps, usually to a 4/4 beat.

Motif – a short phrase of movement that contains within it something capable of being developed.

Opposition – the co-ordination of movement of one side of the body with the other; it is a natural balancing of effort by the body, e.g. when walking and using the right leg and left arm.

Parallel Position – standing, feet slightly apart, with all the toes facing one wall.
- sitting, with the knees facing the ceiling and the legs straight.

Pathways – the pattern made by movements in the air or on the floor.

Phrase – a 'sentence' of movements.

Placement of Weight – for dancers the weight is over the ball of the foot for speed, agility, control and balance.

Plié – a knee bend.

Polka – step, step, step, hop.

Proportion and Balance – these terms apply to the movement content, use of space, number of dancers, all of which contribute to the parts which combine to achieve equilibrium in the whole dance.

Rondo – a musical form, e.g. ABAC, in which one theme recurs interspersed with contrasting themes, i.e. a chorus and verse structure.

Samba – a style of dance and music to a 4/4 beat, often associated with the carnivals of South America.

Sequence – one movement followed by another creates a sequence.

A Skip – a step hop in uneven rhythm.

Spotting – whilst turning the eyes focus on a particular spot in the room for as long as possible; as the head turns, the eyes focus on the same spot again.

Staccato – short and detached style, the opposite of legato.

Style – a manner of dancing or composing dances
e.g. National Style – Cossack, Samba
Personal Style – Graham or Cunningham
Cultural Style – classical ballet

Technique – movement skill.

Tension – stretching without straining the body.

Transition – how a phrase, a movement or shape starts and finishes, and how this relates to what precedes and follows it.

Travel – move from A to B.

Turn Out – the turn out is initiated from rotation in the hips; the knees should be aligned over the toes.

Unison – within a group, the movements take place at the same time.

Unity – a sense of wholeness which is achieved through the sum of the sections in a whole dance or part of a dance.

appendix

Dance Organisations

ADiTi
(National Organization of South
Asian Dancers)
Jacob's Well
Bradford, West Yorkshire BD1
5RW

Arts Council of Great Britain
Dance Department
14 Great Peter Street, London
SW14 3NQ

Arts Council of Northern Ireland
181a Stranwillis Road
Belfast BT9 5DU

Arts Education for a Multi-Cultural
Society
Commonwealth Institute
Kensington High Street
London W8 6NQ

Black Dance Development Trust
Clarence Chambers
4th Floor, Rooms 34–35
39 Corporation Street
Birmingham B4 4LG

Community Dance and Mime
Foundation
School of Arts
Leicester Polytechnic
Scraptoft Campus
Leicester LE7 9SU

Council for Dance Education and
Training
5 Tavistock Place
London WC1H 9SS

Dance and the Child International
Dance Department, Froebel College
Roehampton Institute
Roehampton Lane
London SW15 5J

English Folk Dance and Song
Society
2 Regent's Park Road
London NW1 7AY

National Association of Teachers in
Further and Higher Education
Dance Section
Hamilton House
Mabledon Place
London WC1H 9BH

National Dance Teachers'
Association
Dance Department
Bedford College of Higher
Education
37 Lansdowne Road
Bedford MK40 2BZ

National Resource Centre for
Dance
University of Surrey
Guildford, Surrey GU2 5XH

National Youth Dance Company
35 Gloucester Road
Kew
Richmond, Surrey TW9 3BS

Standing Conference on Dance in
Higher Education
c/o Department of Dance Studies
University of Surrey
Guildford, Surrey GU2 5XH

Scottish Arts Council
12 Manor Place
Edinburgh EH3 7DD

Useful Periodicals

Dance Matters (NDTA publication)
Dancing Times
Dance Theatre Journal (Laban
Centre publication)

Catalogue

Dance Books Ltd
9 Cecil Court
London WC2N 4EZ

They stock books, videos and
cassettes concerned with dance.

Dance Music Tapes

Philip Taylor
55 Gardner St
Glasgow
G11 5DA

Inner Sense Percussion Orchestra
ISPO/Hula
PO Box 20
Levenshulme
Manchester M19 2PZ

(Book and cassette 'Rhythms of
Brazil' – information about carnival
and the roots of samba)

Dance Companies

These all have educational units or
programmes. The following are a
selection of those available:

Adventures in Motion Pictures
c/o Sadlers Wells Theatre
Rosebery Avenue
London EC1R 4TN

Adzido Pan African Dance
Ensemble
The Trade Centre
202–208 New North Road
London N1 7BL

Birmingham Royal Ballet
Birmingham Hippodrome
Thorp Street
Birmingham B5 4AU

Diversions Dance Company
30 Richmond Road
Cardiff CF2 3AS

English National Ballet
Markova House
39 Jay Mews
London SW7 2ES

Irie
The Albany Empire
Douglas Way
Deptford
London SE8 4AG

Kokuma
163 Gerrard St
Lozells, Birmingham B19 2AP

Ludus North-West Dance in
Education Company
Ludus Dance Centre
Assembly Rooms
King Street
Lancaster LA1 1RE

Northern Ballet Theatre
11 Zion Crescent
Hulme Walk, Manchester
M15 5BY

Phoenix Dance Company
3 St Peter's Buildings
St Peter's Square
Leeds LS9 8AH

Rambert Dance Company
94 Chiswick High Road
London W4 1SH

The Royal Ballet
Royal Opera House
Covent Garden, London
WC2E 9DD

Scottish Ballet
261 West Princes Street
Glasgow G4 9EE

Second Stride
Towngate Theatre
Paget Mead
Basildon, Essex
SS14 1DW

Shobana Jeyasingh Dance
Company
Interchange Studios
15 Wilkin Street
London NW5 3NG

Siobhan Davies Company
Riverside Studios
Crisp Road
London W6 9RL

The Kosh
Unit G13A
Belgravia Workshops
157–163 Marlborough Road
London N19 4NF

London Contemporary Dance
Theatre
The Place
17 Duke's Road
London WC1H 9AB

Academic Institutions and Organisations

Useful addresses:

Laban Centre for Movement and
Dance
Laurie Grove
New Cross
London SE14 6NH

University of Surrey
Division of Dance Studies
Guildford
Surrey GU2 5XH

Calouste Gulbenkian Foundation
UK Branch
98 Portland Place
London W1N 4ET

National Foundation for Arts
Education
Department of Arts Education
University of Warwick
Coventry CV4 7AL

BBC School Radio
The Producer
Dance Series
1 Portland Place
London W1A 1AA

References

Best, D. (1985) *Feeling and Reason in the Arts*, Allen and Unwin.

Osborne, H. (1970) *The Art of Appreciation*, Oxford University Press.

Reid, L. A. (1983) 'Aesthetic Knowing,' in Ross, M., *The Arts a Way of Knowing*, Pergamon Press.

Smith, J. M. (1976) *Dance Composition – a practical guide for teachers*, A. & C. Black.

Smith, J. M. (1988) 'Dance as Art Education: New Directions,' in *Young People Dancing – 4th International Conference*, Dance and the Child International, Vol. 1 – Dance Education.

index

Dance Ideas and Frameworks